Maya Ruins of Mexico in Color

Palenque

UNIVERSITY OF OKLAHOMA PRESS Norman

Palenque Uxmal Kabah Sayil
Xlapak Labná Chichén Itzá Cobá Tulum

Maya Ruins of Mexico in Color

by William M. Ferguson

In collaboration with John Q. Royce

Color photographs by **William M. Ferguson** and **John Q. Royce**

Library of Congress Cataloging in Publication Data

Ferguson, William M.
   Maya ruins of Mexico in color.

   Bibliography: P.
   Includes index.
   1.   Mayas--Antiquities.   2.   Mexico--Antiquities.
I.   Royce, John Q., joint author.   II.   Title.
F1435.F4   972   77–9110
ISBN 0–8061–1442–8

foreword

The Maya ruins described in this magnificent book have never actually been "lost." Tulum, for instance, was seen by the first Spanish reconnaissance off the east coast of Yucatán, Chichén Itzá was explored by the sixteenth century bishop, Diego de Landa, and Uxmal was visited by Fray Antonio de Ciudad Real in 1588. Palenque lies in an area continuously occupied by a heavy population of Chol-speaking Mayas, and its investigation began as long ago as the eighteenth century. The Mayas themselves had never forgotten the imposing ceremonial centers of the Yucatán Peninsula, and until recently hunters regularly burned incense to the stelae of Cobá. It was the native Mayas who guided the great nineteenth-century explorers John Lloyd Stephens and Frederick Catherwood to most of the greatest Maya sites, including those shown in this book.

Since their day, there have been hundreds of guidebooks, picture books, and scholarly monographs covering the Maya ruins of Mexico. One would thus think that there remained nothing new to see, describe, or photograph. This conclusion is wrong on two counts. First, the past five years have seen a virtual revolution in our knowledge of the ancient Maya; I am particularly thinking of the exciting new work on the most beautiful of all ruined "cities," Palenque, with its extraordinary dynastic records, and of the recent investigations by Arthur Miller and others on sites of the east coast. These exciting findings have been incorporated in the present text.

But the second factor which makes this book unique is one of perspective. While aerial reconnaissance was inaugurated by Charles A. Lindbergh and Percy Madeira in 1929, I doubt that aerial coverage has been used by anyone so effectively as by William Ferguson and John Royce. The color views taken by them at low altitudes give one a far better idea of Maya buildings and their relationship to one another and to the landscape than any amount of maps and plans. The objection might be raised that the ancient Maya never saw these sites in this way, but after a helicopter flight which I made in 1967 over the famous Olmec center of San Lorenzo in Veracruz, I began to wonder if the native architects and planners did not envision what their creations would look like to a soaring bird.

The sound text and exciting color plates, including both air and ground views, make this a valuable addition to the literature on Maya archaeology, and an authorative guide for the armchair or actual visitor to Mexico's Maya wonders.

Michael D. Coe
Yale University

v

Preface

The Precolumbian Mayas were the most sophisticated people of the New World. These Indians developed a written language, calculated the apparent movement of the sun and moon, developed a calendar of incredible complexity and accuracy, and evolved a vigesimal system of mathematics (including the concept of the zero).

Without the aid of beasts of burden, the wheel, or sophisticated tools, the Mayas constructed magnificent building complexes of rubble, stone, and mortar and decorated them with painting, sculpture, and mosaic.

As this civilization waned and died, its ceremonial centers were abandoned. They were enshrouded as they were abandoned by the encroaching forest and scrub. There are probably hundreds of Maya sites covered by the forests of Mexico, but only a relative few have been cleared and restored, and of these, seven of the most beautiful and magnificent centers of the ancient Mayas of Mexico have been photographed in detail for this book: Palenque, Chichén Itzá, and Uxmal, four smaller sites of the Puuc, near Uxmal—Kabah, Sayil, Xlapak, and Labna—and the east coast sites of Cobá and Tulum.

Palenque in Chiapas and Uxmal in the Puuc area of Yucatán were Classic Maya sites that were abandoned perhaps six hundred years before the arrival of the Spaniards. Chichén Itzá in Yucatán was occupied for several more centuries into the Maya Post-Classic period and displays the art and architecture which resulted from the fusion of the Mexican (Toltec) culture and the culture of the Classic Mayas.

In this volume are about 200 color plates, many of the photographs taken from the air. The aerial photographs give a perspective to the Maya ruins which enables the viewer to visualize the relationship of each building to the site as a whole. The material is current, as all of the photographs, with a few exceptions, were taken in the mid-1970's.

Interwoven with the explanatory material that directly relates to each photograph of an area, structure, or artifact are indications of the Maya way of life during the period A.D. 500 to 1200. In addition, there is a brief introduction to Maya culture with a summary of the origins, history, religious rites, sacrifices, intellectual achievements, agriculture, and social order, together with maps and charts and a section on the Maya order of architecture.

Recent research has immeasurably broadened our knowledge of the Ancient Mayas. Much material from texts only recently considered unimpeachable is now either suspect or actually outdated, and the new material is just being assembled and is not yet published. Much of the information given here is a synthesis of the data obtained by personal communication with Mayanists of various disciplines. Within the past few years, great progress has been made in the translation of Maya glyph writing. At Palenque, particularly, there has been a breakthrough in the correlation of dates, the understanding of the names and lineages of rulers, and interpretation of iconography. Some of this new material is published here for the first time.

Palenque is located at the edge of the rain forest in the Chiapas Mountains, where the verdure is always a lush green. Yucatán is brown in the dry season and verdant during the rainy months. The photographs of the Puuc (the area south of Mérida, Yucatán, where Uxmal is located) and of Chichén Itzá taken in March reveal a backdrop of dry-season landscape in colors of brown and beige. The aerial views taken in June show the country in the vibrant green of summer.

The photographs made the publication of this book possible. Maya scholars saw in these color photographs—particularly the aerials—depictions of the inherent grandeur of the Maya centers that they had appreciated academically but had never viewed from this perspective. Moreover, they could see that pictures in color portray the natural beauty of the architecture and the intricacy of the iconography in a way impossible with black and white.

The authors, who are not archaeologists or anthropologists, were given instruction, assistance, and encouragement by experts in the field. To them we express our deep appreciation.

Michael D. Coe read the manuscript and wrote a foreword; Jeff Kowalski, authority on the iconography of Uxmal, checked the material on the Puuc area; Arthur G. Miller read and corrected the text on Cobá, Tulum, and Chichén Itzá; Tatiana Proskouriakoff gave encouragement in many ways; and Linda Schele by personal communication furnished unpublished data on Palenque, read the text, and gave advice and direction. She also generously provided certain drawings of her own for inclusion. We wish to express our thanks to the Instituto National de Anthropologia E Historia of Mexico which granted permission to take the photographs.

To other authorities, past and present, we want to express our gratitude for both inspiration and tangible help, in the use of textual materials and illustrations. Unless noted otherwise, the photographs are our own, with the especially notable exception of one generously provided by Merle Greene Robertson. All other illustrations from other sources are acknowledged, with thanks, with credit lines.

We also extend our thanks to William M. Ferguson III, a scholar in the field of English literature, for reading the manuscript, and to his wife, Jane M. Ferguson, for her assistance as proofreader, draftsman, and source of information on the vagaries of architectural terminology.

William M. Ferguson
John Q. Royce
Wellington, Kansas
August 1, 1977

Contents

MAPS

ix

Maya Ruins of Mexico in Color

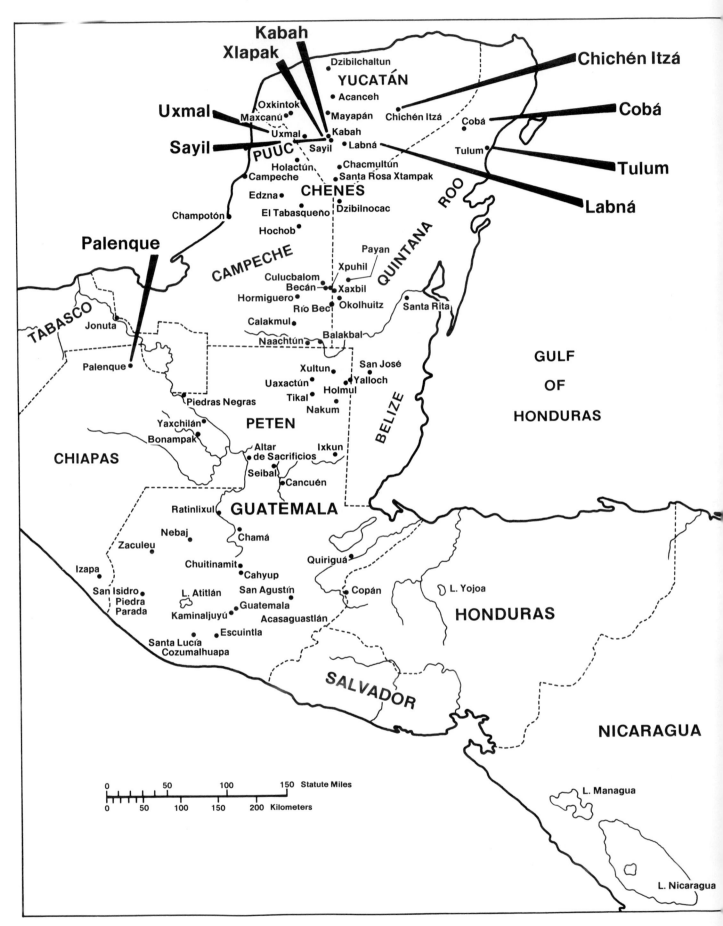

The Maya Area

Introduction to the Mayas

The antecedents of the Ancient Maya Indians were northeastern Asiatics who migrated to the North American continent across the Alaskan land-bridge (Bering Strait) beginning probably more than eleven thousand years ago. They gradually overspread North, Central, and South America, those we now call Mayas settling in the Mesoamerican area. There, with the domestication of corn (maize), they began the transition from hunting and collecting to cultivation during the period 6500 to 1000 B.C.

Until recently, the Maya civilization, as we think of it today, was considered to have arisen from a synthesis of Mesoamerican peoples, including especially the Olmec civilization of the Gulf Coast lowlands (1200–100 B.C.). Norman Hammond, however, reports that his work, which was begun in 1975 at Cuello in Belize, "has pushed the beginnings of the Maya Formative (or Preclassic) period back by more than 1,500 years, from about 900 B.C. to perhaps as long ago as 2600 B.C. (Hammond, 1977: 116)." Thus the Maya culture may be among the oldest settled societies in the New World. By the time of the Classic period (A.D. 200) the people we call Mayas occupied a large part of Mesoamerica: present Guatemala, except portions of the coastal strip on the Pacific; Belize; the western portion of Honduras; and, in Mexico, the states of Yucatán, Campeche, Quintana Roo, Tabasco (except for an area on the west), and the eastern part of Chiapas.

Physical Appearance

So far as can be determined, the ancient Mayas had complexions of copper-brown with straight black or dark brown hair; they were short in stature—the men probably were no more than five feet one inch tall on the average, and the women smaller. They had rather long arms and small hands and feet. In the Maya Classic period, sloped foreheads and large noses were considered personally decorative, and parents deformed the skulls of young children by fastening boards around their foreheads. Adults of both sexes were often tatooed and scarified and had their front teeth filed. Bishop Diego de Landa (1524–1579), whose writings are one of the principal sources of our knowledge of Maya culture, said of the women: "They are not white but of a yellowish brown color, caused more by the sun and by their constant bathing than from nature. . . . They had a custom of filing their teeth leaving them like the teeth of a saw, and this they considered elegant. . . . They pierced their ears in order to put in earrings like their husbands (Tozzer, 1941: 125–26)."

History

Fitting a culture into a time framework is an inexact science at best, but J. Eric S. Thompson, in his *Rise and Fall of Maya Civilization*

3

(Norman, 1954, 1966), gave a synopsis of Maya history that is so succinct and clear that it seems inadvisable to attempt to better it. It is the basis of the following summary.

Maya history can be divided into four distinct periods: Formative (c. 1500 B.C.—A.D. 200), Classic (c. A.D. 200–925), Mexican (A.D. 925–1200), and Mexican Absorption (A.D. 1200–1540).

During the *Formative* period, there was a rise of agricultural civilizations on approximately the same cultural levels and with essentially the same religion throughout Mesoamerica. Pyramids were built, and a hierarchy probably began to emerge. Good plain pottery and figurines were fashioned, along with elementary hieroglyphic writing and the simpler components of the calendar. Development was strong on the Pacific Coast and in the Guatemalan highlands. It is not certain exactly what was occurring in the lowlands, but by the end of the period the Mayas of the Petén and Yucatán were erecting pyramids, although their sculpture was still largely in the styles they had shared with their non-Maya neighbors.

The *Classic* period may be subdivided into Early (A.D. 200–625), Florescence (A.D. 625–800), and Collapse (A.D. 800–925). There was, of course, no sharp division from the Formative period, but there was an expansion and perfection of architecture, art, and the stela cult. Corbel vaulting was fully developed, hieroglyphic monuments were being erected at many Maya centers, and Maya art was developing its characteristic features. This period represented a cultural peak for highland Maya cities, though toward the close of the phase, a period of quiescence is noted in the lowlands.

The florescent phase embraced the greatest era of sculpture, hieroglyphic writing, and building for the lowland Mayas. Fine painted pottery, mold-made figurines, and lapidary work combined with great progress in astronomy and mathematics. The number of cere-monial centers and stelae increased greatly. On the other hand, there was a decline in the Guatemala highlands.

Then came the period of the collapse of cities in the central area, the real reasons are not known, though Thompson believes they could include reaction to the barbarians from the north of Mexico. The infiltration of Mexican influence in western Yucatán affected some Puuc cities, and many of them were abandoned. In the central area it meant a return to conditions existing in the Formative period, perhaps with a village or villages as a political unit. And there was growing Mexican influence in Yucatán.

In the *Mexican* period, Mexicanized groups conquered Chichén Itzá, introducing some architectural features and art from Tula, worship of Quetzalcoatl and other Mexican gods, and warfare to obtain sacrificial victims for the sun. The use of metal, the making of plumbate pottery, and the use of turquoise were important features. The fall of Chichén Itzá signaled the end of the period.

The period of *Mexican Absorption* was marked by the Mayapán "empire" in Yucatán and the dominance of the Quichés in the highlands of Guatemala. Ruling groups abandoned their Mexican culture, except for warfare, and gradually became Maya in speech and religion. The ceremonial centers became real cities, and architecture and the arts became decadent. After revolts against Mayapán and the Quichés in the highlands of Guatemala, the Mayas were governed by small independent chieftains who continually warred among themselves. The cultural decline continued until Maya civilization was cut short by the Spanish Conquest in 1525 and 1541. Itzás in Tayasal, however, remained independent until 1697.

As has been indicated, the real reasons for the demise of the Classic Maya civilization are not known, though many theories have been advanced. Michael D. Coe, in *The Maya* (New York, 1966) has summarized the situation:

Almost the only fact surely known about the downfall of the Classic Maya civilization is that it really happened. All the rest is pure conjecture. The sad story can clearly be read in the failure of centre after centre to put up commemorative stelae following the opening of Baktun 10 of Maya history, in the first half of the ninth century of our era. The katun ending date 10.3.0.0.0 (AD 889) was celebrated by inscriptions at only three sites. And the very last Long Count date to be recorded anywhere was the katun ending 10.4.0.0.0, incised on a jade from a site in southern Quintana Roo. Thus, by the beginning of the tenth century the Classic Maya civilization had been extinguished in the Central Area, and we may be sure that most of its great centres were by then deserted, abandoned to the encroachments of the waiting forests. To the north, the Puuc sites may have been occupied until their overthrow by Toltec armies in the latter decades of the century.

Not only the demise of the Classic centres must be explained, but also the disappearance of the Maya people throughout most of the Central Area. Among the causes for these events which have been advanced are agricultural collapse, epidemic diseases like yellow fever, invasion by foreigners from Mexico, social revolution, forced evacuation by the early Toltec rulers of Yucatán, and even earthquakes and an unbalanced sex ratio! In desperation, some scholars have proposed varying combinations of all these factors, but it must be realized that there is little or no proof that any one of them prevailed. The agricultural collapse theory, for instance, presupposes that the savannahs of the Petén resulted from over-exploitation of the land by Maya farmers, but we have seen that these grasslands were there before the people.

Nevertheless, by the mid-ninth century there are indications of Mexican involvement with Maya sites, particularly those in the western part of the region. Seibal, for instance, erected a series of stelae early in Baktun 10 which show costume details and Tlaloc masks which look almost Toltec. It may be that the lowland Maya were already so weak from other causes that Mexicans could intrude without opposition into the Central Area. But until we can read the last inscriptions we shall never know what actually went on (Coe, 1966: 114).

Until recently Post-Classic building at Chichén Itzá has been attributed to the "Toltecs," who were a Nahua-speaking people who settled in the Valley of Mexico at Tula about A.D. 900. According to legend, the king of the Toltecs, bearing the name of the god Quetzalcoatl, was forced to leave Tula with his followers, most probably in A.D. 987, and thereafter migrated to the Gulf Coast. From the Gulf Coast the Toltecs were thought to have attacked and conquered the Mayas of Yucatán and set up a capital in Chichén Itzá under the leadership of Topiltzin Quetzalcoatl (Kukulcán).

Recent research, however, indicates that there was Mexican influence in Yucatán far earlier than A.D. 987; in fact, probably at least two hundred years before the founding of Chichén Itzá. Also, it is now established that Chichén was governed by an alliance of several Mexican-influenced peoples.

It is not yet known definitively which peoples made up the invasions, when they arrived, or where they came from, but it is certain that they were not all Toltecs, and some of them may have been from the heavily Mexican-influenced "buffer zone" of the present-day Tabasco area. In this volume we refer to the invading peoples of Yucatán as "Mexicans." We also know that the invaders were soon influenced by Maya culture and became "Mayanized." For these reasons we refer to the Post-Classic peoples of Chichén Itzá as "Mayanized-Mexicans."

Divisions

The ancient Maya civilization was divided into three general areas.

The Pacific Coast and the Guatemala highlands comprised the area which led the Pre-Classic development of the Maya civilization (300 B.C.–A.D. 300) and was the area of transition from the Olmec culture to the Maya. Here also the cultural impact from Teoti-

5

huacán (in the Valley of Mexico) during the early Classic period caused these Mayas to develop separately and somewhat apart from the Central Maya cultural expression.

The Central Maya area was the rain forest which extends from Copán in Honduras through the Petén region of Guatemala to what is now Belize, Quintana Roo, Campeche, Tabasco, and Chiapas. Major Maya sites in this area which have been excavated are, from south to north: Copán, Quiriguá, Tikal, Uaxactún, Yaxchilán, Piedras Negras, and Palenque. The principal elements that distinguish the Classic Mayas were developed here, i.e., temples with corbel vaulting, hieroglyphic writing, and the Long Count calendar.

The third area is in the northern Yucatán peninsula. Here the major excavated sites are Etzna, Uxmal (and nearby Kabah, Sayil, Xlapak and Labná), Chichén Itzá, Dzibilchaltún, Mayapán, and Tulum. The Post-Classic Mayas occupied Tulum following the collapse of Chichén Itzá.

Agriculture

The civilization of the New World was founded on the cultivation of maize or Indian corn (zea mays). The domestication of corn, says Michael Coe, was "the most important discovery ever attained by the American Indians. For this plant created and fed native New World civilization (1968: 32)." This corn, plus beans and squash, formed the basis of the Mesoamerican diet.

Maya agriculture probably included techniques very similar to those currently employed by the descendants of the Mayas now living in Yucatán. The method is called swidden or slash-and-burn agriculture. It comprised cutting the trees and underbrush in a section of the forest, burning the dried trees and brush, planting, and harvesting. Corn, of course, was the primary crop, with squash and beans generally planted in the same field,

as well as pumpkins, chili peppers, tomatoes, yucca, and sweet potatoes. The basic tools were the sharp planting stick (xul) and the stone axe (baat). When the corn was ripe, the heads were bent over so that the husks would shed the rain and the corn would keep until harvested. The milpa (cornfield), if continuously planted, produced less and less corn each year so that after a few years it became necessary to abandon one milpa and clear and burn another field.

In recent years, serious questions have been raised concerning whether primitive swidden agriculture could have supported the number of people now believed to have lived in the area inhabited by the ancient Mayas. This doubt has led to speculation that the Mayas probably also used more sophisticated methods of cultivation. Professor B. L. Turner II, of the University of Oklahoma, and others have studied the remains of Maya large-scale hillside terracing in southern Yucatán and their "raised fields" (artificial platforms of soil in the flooded lowland areas). He suggests that the Petén, during the Classic period, may have been cultivated with the same intensity as central Ohio is today (La Fay, 1975: 733).

Food

The basic food, maize, was prepared by boiling or soaking it in lime water. The wet maize was then ground on a metate (a stone slab) with a mano (a round grinding stone), and the resulting paste was mixed with water to make pozole, which was either a liquid or a cake now known as a tortilla. Then, as now, the tortilla was cooked on a flat pottery griddle and eaten with beans or chili.

The Classic Mayas raised dogs for food and domesticated the turkey and ducks. The Yucatán Mayas were beekeepers. In addition, the Mayas ate the flesh of deer, wild boars, birds, fish, iguanas, rabbits, turtles, and insects. Intoxicating beverages were made with a honey base.

Bishop Landa described the diet of the Mayas in the sixteenth century thus: "They started the day by drinking a hot gruel of finely ground maize. During the day they drank liquids which were either watered-down gruel or a foaming beverage made from ground maize and cacao or from ground maize spiced with chili peppers. At night they ate stews of vegetables and deer meat, fish or birds."

Clothing

Bishop Landa tells us that Maya clothing at the time of the Conquest "was a band of the width of a hand, which served them for drawers and breeches. They wound it several times around the waist, so that one end fell in front and one end behind, and these ends the women made with a great deal of care and with feather-work. They wore large square *mantas* and tied them over their shoulders. They wore sandals of hemp or of the dry un-tanned skin of the deer, and they wore no other garments (Tozzer, 1941: 89)."

The nobles had much finer garb. Their sandals and mantles were very elaborate, and they wore sleeveless jackets made of jaguar or deer skins. Their headdresses were variously made of the feathers of toucans, parrots, hummingbirds, herons, and macaws, and the long, beautiful feathers of the quetzal bird.

The evolution in the costumes of the nobles can be traced through progressive styles on stelae. In the Classic period, the basic garment was the loin cloth that terminated as an apron in the front. Some of the sculptured figures are depicted wearing short skirts, others long skirts made of cloth or skins. The stela figures wore elaborate headdresses of feathers and jade. In addition, the figures are shown with ear ornaments, necklaces, belts, arm and leg ornaments, and sandals.

Tools

Maya technology was neolithic. Metal was apparently unknown in the Classic period, and in Post-Classic times it was used primarily for ornaments—there were few metal tools. All the building stones were cut and dressed and the sculpture was executed with stone tools. The plumb line was used and possibly levels and squaring devices. There were no wheeled vehicles and no animals available for motive power. The Mayas no doubt had ropes and may have used logs for rollers. Construction of the pyramids and rubble-filled buildings was accomplished by manpower alone, probably with the tumpline. The illustration depicts a deity carrying a burden by means of a tumpline.

Deity Using a Tumpline

Stone tools were made of flint, obsidian, granite, limestone, and quartzite. The percussion-flaked flint core was probably the general utility tool for masonry work and stone dressing. Other stones were hafted for use as chisels or axes. In addition, there were flint and obsidian tools for scraping, polishing, and plastering. The tools required to work jade probably included hammer-stones, grinding stones, rasps, and solid drills. Saws of wood and hollow drills of reed or birdbone were used with abrasives. Incising was probably done with jade or flint tools.

Transportation and Trade

Known ancient Maya roads *(sacbeob)* vary in length from less than one mile to more than sixty miles. They were about fifteen feet wide, were covered with lime cement, and had sides of roughly dressed stones. In fact, a road roller in the form of a limestone cylinder, requiring fifteen men to move, was found near Cobá. It is believed that these roads were primarily ceremonial ways rather than paths of travel. The bulk of the commerce by land probably went by rough trails through the brush and jungle.

Travel was largely on foot except for wealthy merchants and nobles who rode in litters carried by two or more men. Wooden poles which rested on the shoulders of a carrier in front and one in the rear supported the litter.

Much transportation was by water. The network of rivers carried the commerce throughout the central Maya area, and there was a large volume of commerce by sea around the Yucatán peninsula. Indeed, throughout all Precolumbian history, trade and commerce were carried on among the various Mesoamerican peoples.

There were trade routes on land and sea. Columbus, on his fourth voyage, described a Maya vessel which he encountered carrying passengers and a cargo which included "cotton mantles, *huipils* [blouses] and loincloths, all with multicolor designs, *macanas* [wooden swords with pieces of flint or obsidian glued into slots down each side], little copper axes and bells, plates and forges to melt copper, razors and knives of copper, and hatchets of a sharp, bright-yellow stone with wooden hafts and large quantities of cacao (Thompson, 1966: 221)." These were goods of the Post-Classic period, for the Classic Mayas did not utilize copper.

Yucatán was the source of salt for Mesoamerica and also exported honey, cotton mantles, and slaves. Quetzal feathers, jade, flint, shells, and obsidian were traded. Pieces of obsidian the size of a fist were bartered.

From this obsidian core, a sharp cutting edge could be separated by one well-placed blow, producing a razor of knife.

Maya currency used in trade included the cacao bean, spondylus shell beads, or jade, beans being the universal currency of the entire area. A load of beans contained about 24,000 individual beans, which in the early sixteenth century was "worth about $9.50 on the isthmus, but nearly double that in Mexico City (Thompson, 1966: 220)."

Government and Society

Throughout the ancient Maya realm civil power was in the hands of hereditary nobles. Thus the Mayas were governed by the elite group of a class society in which ancestry and lineage were of primary importance. Palenque, we know, was governed by a series of rulers from one family who exercised a combination of civil and ecclesiastical authority. They portrayed themselves as the deity identified as God K. In the Post-Classic era of Chichén Itzá the Mexican warrior class wielded a porportionately greater share of power than the priests. In Yucatán, at the time of the Conquest, each area was governed by a *halach uinic* (real man) who inherited his post in the male line.

Society was complex. At the top were the aristocracy of civil, military, and religious leaders. Next in the social order were the artisans and merchants, and at the bottom were the peasants who lived in the nearby countryside and raised the crops.

Archaeological evidence from the Classic period, especially at Palenque, suggests high social status for the nobles. The burials, particularly, indicate the wealth of the kings and nobles. And the magnificent architecture and sculpture demonstrate that the priests and nobles had a large force of laborers who could be called upon for the heavy work and a corps of expert artisans for the design and art.

Warfare

Sylvanus G. Morley, who wrote his classic *The Ancient Maya* in 1946, believed the Mayas to be a peaceful people and suggested "a near absence of war" and "comparative tranquility in the central Maya area during Classic times (Morley and Brainerd, 1956: 58)." But modern research has changed this view, as the following statement in 1966 by Michael Coe attests:

The Maya were obsessed with war. The Annals of the Cakchiquels and the Popol Vuh speak of little but intertribal conflict among the highlanders, while the 16 states of Yucatán were constantly battling with each other over boundaries and lineage honour. To this sanguinary record we must add the testimony of the Classic monuments and their inscriptions. From these and from the eye-witness descriptions of the *conquistadores* we can see how Maya warfare was waged. The *holcan* or 'braves' were the footsoldiers; they wore cuirasses of quilted cotton or of tapir hide and carried thrusting spears with flint points, darts-with-*atlatl*, and in late Post-Classic times, the bow-and-arrow. Hostilities typically began with an unannounced guerrilla raid into the enemy camp to take captives, but more formal battle opened with the dreadful din of drums, whistles, shell trumpets, and war cries. On either side of the war leaders and the idols carried into the combat under the care of the priests were the two flanks of infantry, from which rained darts, arrows, and stones flung from slings. Once the enemy had penetrated into home territory however, irregular warfare was substituted, with ambuscades and all kinds of traps. Lesser captives ended up as slaves, but the nobles and war leaders had their hearts torn out on the sacrificial stone (Coe, 1966: 147).

Deities and Religion

The Mayas apparently believed in cyclical creations and destructions of the earth and mankind. It is thought that they believed that the universe in which they lived was created in 3114 B.C., but we do not know how long this cycle was to have continued. The earth was conceived of as being flat and four-cornered. The sky was thought to be multilayered and supported at the corners by four Bacabs, each direction having a color association: east, red; north, white; south, yellow; and west, black. The sky was supported by trees of different colors and species with the green ceiba tree in the center. There were thirteen layers of heaven each with its own god and nine layers of the underworld ruled by nine lords of the night.

At the end of each day the sun was swallowed by one head of the two-headed earth monster, to be regurgitated in the east the next morning from the other head.

The Maya universe was filled with a great number of deities, perhaps even thousands, considering the various aspects of each deity. "Each was not only one but four individuals, separately assigned to the color-directions (Coe, 1966: 151)." Many had counterparts in the opposite sex, and each astronomical god had an underworld counterpart. As each god died, he passed beneath the earth to reappear again in the heavens in the same way as the sun.

God K   *Jester God*

From Robertson, *Primera Mesa Redonda de Palenque, I*

9

From Coe, *The Maya*

*Gods of the Maya pantheon with their name glyphs, from the Dresden Codex.
a, Death God; b, Chaac, the Rain God; c, North Star God; d, Itzamná; e, Maize
God; f, Sun God; g, Young Moon Goddess; h, Bolon Dzacab; i, Ek Chuab, the
Merchant God; j, Ixchel, Goddess of Medicine and Childbirth.*

The rulers of Palenque—and perhaps rulers of other Maya areas—were considered deities in life and in death. God K and the Jester god have been identified as closely connected with rulership, and God K has been identified with the Aztec "Smoking Mirror" god whose name is Tezcatlipoca.

In the Puuc area there are many masks with a long, curved snout which some authorities have identified as the rain god, Chaac (or Chac). Chaac's characteristics include a long nose, two downward curling fangs, and a headdress of quetzal feathers.

Ubiquitous at Chichén Itzá (and in some instances in the Puuc area) are representations of the Mexican god Quetzalcoatl (the feathered serpent) who was known to the Mayas as Kukulcán.

Maya religion was not based on a contrast of good and evil, and apparently most of the Maya deities were considered to embody a duality of good and evil. The god of rain, for example, was probably considered benevolent as long as the rains came in the normal amounts at normal times, but the same god became malevolent when an area was struck by a hurricane. By the same token the sun god was probably considered perverse during periods of drought.

If Maya and Aztec religions were similar, man was obligated to support the god by sacrifices of incense, food, and blood. The priests had the responsibility for the relationship of the Mayas to the gods and, in addition, according to Landa, they directed the "computation of the years, months, and days, the festivals and the ceremonies, the administration of the sacraments, the fateful days and seasons, their methods of divination and their prophecies, events and the cures of diseases, and their antiquities and how to read and write the letters and characters (quoted in Coe, 1966: 153)."

Ritual acts were governed by the calendar,

10

and the details were directed by it. Rituals involved bathing, abstinence from food and sexual contact, and sacrifice. Self-mutilation was carried out by piercing the ears, cheeks, lips, tongue, and penis and spattering the blood on the face or body of the representation of a god. Animal and human sacrifices were performed, the human sacrificial victims generally being prisoners of war, slaves, or children. Special rites were performed in connection with military campaigns as well as on behalf of hunters, farmers, fishermen, and artisans.

Numeration and the Computation of Time

The ancient Mayas were excellent mathematicians, early developing a system of numeration which included the concept of zero. They utilized both bar-and-dot geometric numerals and a system of personified numerals in somewhat the same way that we can indicate a number by using an arabic figure, or by writing it in words. The Mayas combined three symbols—the dot with a numerical value of 1, a bar with a numerical value of 5, and a shell to indicate 0. These symbols were organized into a vertical vigesimal position system. In our system the positions to the left of the decimal point increase by tens. In the Maya system the values of the positions increase by twenties from bottom to top.

The computation of time constituted a high achievement. The Maya Long Count was a consecutive count of elapsed days from a fixed date in the past. In our culture we use the birth of Christ as a starting point. The Mayas utilized 13.0.0.0.0, 4 Ahau 8 Cumhu, which was the beginning of the last great cycle and has been calculated as August 11, 3114 B.C. (Thompson correlation). The 13 refers to baktuns (20 katuns or 144,000 days), the zeros refer to katuns (20 tuns or 7,200 days), tuns (18 uinals or 360 days), uinals (20 kins or 20 days), and kins (1 day).

The first nineteen numbers are as follows:

0	🐚	11	⚊̇
1	•	12	⚌
2	••	13	
3	•••	14	
4	••••	15	
5	▬	16	
6	▬̇	17	
7	▬̈	18	
8	▬ •••	19	
9	▬ ••••		
10	▬▬		

The vigesimal count may be illustrated as follows:

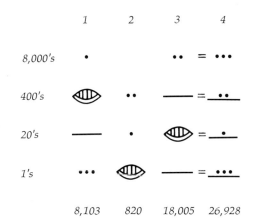

Note that column four is the sum of the three preceding columns and was obtained by combining the bars and dots of columns one, two, and three.

From Thompson, *The Rise and Fall of Maya Civilization*

Computation of Time

The Mayas used a Calendar Round of 52 years which consisted of two permutating cycles, one of 260 days, the other a vague year of 365 days. The 260-day count meshed with a 365-day solar year composed of 18 months of 20 days each with 5 unlucky days added at the end. Each day was considered to be a god and had its own omens and associations. The 20-day periods were a "kind of perpetual fortune-telling machine guiding the destinies of the Maya (Coe, 1966: 55)."

The Mayas living in the Guatemala highlands, who were under Olmec influence, began using their calendar in its final form by the first century B.C., and usage gradually spread to the Petén area. The Long Count system was based on elapsed days, so that it was accurate over great periods of time. In addition, the Mayas faced the problem of co-ordinating their lunar calendar with the solar calendar. About A.D. 682 the Mayas at Copán began calculating with the formula 149 moons =4,400 days, a time-computing system that was eventually adopted by most of the other Maya centers.

The texts in the Group of the Cross in Palenque suggest that the Palencanos were interested in calculating the accumulated error in the 365-day calendar which produced a one-day drift every four solar years. Some of the dates in the Group of the Cross are very near to the amount of time (1508 years of 365 days and 1507 years of 365.2422 days) that it takes for a day to drift entirely around the 365-day calendar to return to its original position in the solar year.

Astronomy

Astronomy was of great interest to Maya scholars, who recognized that the planet Venus was both a morning and an evening star. Many generations of observations and record keeping were required for the Mayas finally to arrive at the figure of 584 days for the Venus year—an error of only one day in 6,000 years. These astronomers also evolved tables for predicting when (but not where) solar eclipses might be visible, and they calculated the lunar revolution to average 29.53020 days as compared with the actual average of 29.53059. Their calculations often went millions of years into the past or the future. Very often they deliberately calculated the intervals between contemporary and ancient dates so that both occupied the same station in several cycles; that is, cycles of the moon, Venus, the sun, eclipses, and non-astronomical cycles not yet fully understood.

Hieroglyphic Writing

The Mayas "alone among all the native people of the New World were fully literate; that is, they had a script sufficiently developed so they could write down anything in their language (Coe, 1968: 123)." The system used hieroglyphs, and while the script has not been deciphered, the calendrical portions and texts on stelae and reliefs, which portray historical events such as births, deaths, marriages, conquests, and transfers of power among rulers, have been translated (Coe, 1968: 122). Progress in deciphering is slow because there is no comparative translation or Maya equivalent to the Rosetta stone; however, great progress has been made in recent years by Linda Schele, Peter Mathews, David Kelley, Floyd Lounsbury, and Merle Green Robertson in deciphering the glyphs of rulers with their lineages and dates at Palenque. This was made possible by an earlier breakthrough by Tatiana Pros-

From Robertson, *Primera Mesa Redonda de Palenque, I*

Panel from Temple of Inscriptions, Palenque

13

kouriakoff, Heinrich Berlin, J. Eric S. Thompson, and others.

In addition to the stelae, bas reliefs, and incised panels, three books of the Mayas have survived: the Codex Dresden, the Codex Madrid, and the Codex Paris. Many others were burned by the Spaniards, as Bishop Landa recorded in the sixteenth century: "We found a large number of books of these characters and, as they contained nothing in which there were not to be seen superstition and lies of the devil, we burned them all which they regretted to an amazing degree and which caused them much affliction (quoted in Tozzer, 1941: 77)."

Sculpture

For a thousand years, Maya artists created sculptured figures, using limestone, sandstone, stucco, wood, clay, and jade, most of the items displaying a basic cultural unity. The "Maya sculptors of the Classic era were Stone Age professionals moving from one site to another as demand required," creating the magnificent artifacts so much admired by twentieth-century man (Kubler, 1975: 161). This sculpture will be discussed further in connection with individual sites and buildings.

The style of the altars and the relief sculpture of priests and warriors of the Classic Mayas were replaced between the eighth and tenth centuries with the serpent-mask mosaic forms and the panels of abstract ornaments found at Uxmal and other Puuc sites. This shift in style and emphasis is comparable to the stylistic change from Romanesque to Gothic in European sculpture which climaxed in the twelfth century.

Although the sculpture of Chichén Itzá reflects the secular influence of the Mexicans and is considered a new era in Maya art following the end of the Classic period, it still represents evolution. The Jaguar Throne found in the substructure of the Castillo is a figure in the round, which evidences a Maya Classic origin, and the "small caryatid figures sup-porting tables or benches perhaps relate to older Maya traditions of sky-bearing personages represented in relief (Kubler, 1975: 201)."

Outside the Maya tradition are the chacmool figures from Chichén, fourteen of which have been found. This art form is thought to have accompanied the various Mexican invasions into the lowland Maya area. There is also no Maya precedent for the standard bearers. The full feathered serpent is rare in Classic Maya art, but the paired serpent-columns of the Castillo, Temple of the Warriors, and the Temple of the Jaguars at Chichén may have Puuc antecedents but not in so massive a form. The heads of the serpents at the base of the columns next to the doorway of the Temple of the Jaguars "are the largest single carved stones at Chichén, weighing 7 1/8 tons each, [and], were re-used, after having been part of an older, now vanished structure (Kubler, 1975: 202)."

Architecture

The spectacular architectural achievements of the Mayas have long been the subject of attention and admiration. Maya architecture had certain features in common regardless of location and time:

1. A rubble- or earth-filled substructure subdivided into terraced levels;
2. One or more stairways leading from plaza spaces to the temple above;
3. Corbel vaults;
4. Stucco veneer over the stone masonry;
5. Roof combs;
6. Exterior and interior relief sculpture;
7. Frontality in temple architecture.

Modifications of both style and construction techniques appeared from area to area and from one period to another. Some of these differences and common features are discussed below in relation to the sites pictured in this volume. Additional details are given in the descriptions of the various sites and individual buildings.

Palenque: The Palencano Mayas developed a unique technical variation on the corbel-vault structural system used by the Classic Mayas. The two outer corbelled walls are not independently balanced as in other Maya architecture; instead, the two outer walls above the doors lean against the center wall. This structural innovation allowed for thinner bearing walls, much wider and more numerous doors, and the incorporation of a greater volume of internal space. As a result, the interiors of the temples of Palenque are more open, better lighted, and better ventilated than those of other Maya sites.

Because the sculptures of Palenque were mounted on the interior walls of the temples, both inscriptional and pictorial information is far more detailed and extensive than at other Maya sites. Plaster sculpture, the major medium of architectural sculpture, became an elaborate and refined art form of great technological and aesthetic achievement. Much of the decoration was stucco, the stucco figures constructed by molding the naked figure, then adding the clothing.

The mansard effect was obtained by the sloping surface of the exterior walls which roughly parallels the slope of the interior vaults; the sloping surface is joined to the vertical lower walls by means of a continuous stringcourse which was altered to form a projecting cornice molding. The roof comb served only to enhance the visual height of the building and perhaps to stabilize the independently balanced center wall.

The Temple of the Cross, shown here, exemplifies the two parallel vaults and the sloping walls which follow the slope of the interior vault.

The technique of employing two parallel galleries or vaults is common to most Classic Maya architecture. But a unique characteristic of Palencano architecture was the addition of the concept of the inward-sloping walls, there-

From Thompson, *The Rise and Fall of Maya Civilization*

Temple of the Cross, Palenque

by placing weight on the central wall, which made possible a reduction in the mass of the front bearing wall. This system, plus the cross vault and the weight-releasing devices (formed by the Moorish-looking openings) seen in this illustration substantially reduced the mass of stone and rubble above door lintel level and

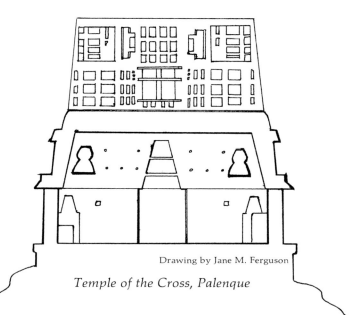

Drawing by Jane M. Ferguson

Temple of the Cross, Palenque

enabled the builders to incorporate much wider openings along the front of the structure.

In addition to the temple-pyramid and range-type (palace) structures at Palenque, there is the unique tower which is thought to have been constructed as an observation platform. It is a square-base building upon which were constructed four stories with four large door-type openings on each floor.

Considered from the point of view of the arrangement of the buildings and their relationship one to another and to the center as a whole, Palenque is far more closely knit and livable than its counterparts at Uxmal and Chichén Itzá. In Yucatán the Puuc Mayas and the Maya Mexicans spread their buildings around open plazas in a grandiose manner, whereas Pacal and his successors retained a closely integrated system of construction at Palenque.

Uxmal: The Pyramid of the Magician at Uxmal exhibits a propensity on the part of Maya builders to construct buildings over existing structures. Here Temple I was constructed at ground level and four temples were added subsequently, the last one being Temple V (or the House of the Magician), which was built on top of the pyramid. This structure is also unique because of its oval substructure

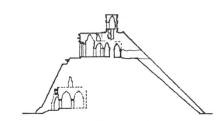

From Kubler, *Art and Architecture of Ancient America,* 2d ed.

House of the Magician Cross-section

and the Chenes characteristics of Temple IV.

The Nunnery complex comprises an open-corner quadrangle of four buildings. Viewed from the Palace of the Governor, all four are visible because the south building is at a lower level than the other three and the north building sits on a platform higher than the others. The style is Puuc with stone mosaic decorations on the upper façade. The decorative style at Uxmal differs from that of Palenque. At Uxmal, stone-mosaic façades are used rather than stucco decoration. Stucco is not unknown at Uxmal, however, several of the older buildings being decorated with stucco. The bearing walls of the Puuc buildings are vertical (often with a negative batter) and do not follow the angle of the inner vault as do the buildings at Palenque.

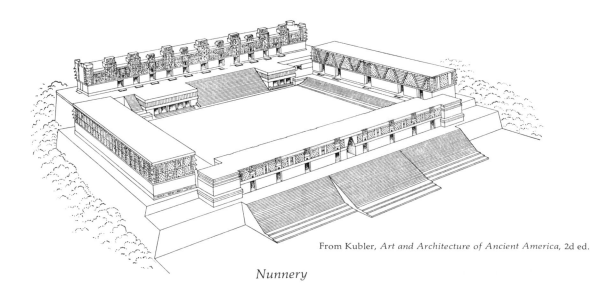

From Kubler, *Art and Architecture of Ancient America,* 2d ed.

Nunnery

16

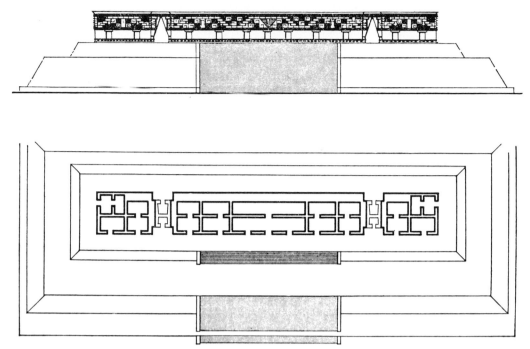

House of the Governor Cross-section and Floor Plan

Sylvanus G. Morley considered the corbel-vaulted masonry buildings to be an archaeologically diagnostic characteristic of the Classic Mayas (Morley and Brainerd, 1956: 40). The arch bears no weight as it was merely a device for preserving a relatively small open space within a core of cement and rubble. The architecture of the Mayas was, like that of the ancient Greeks, outward looking—to be viewed from the outside.

The House of the Governor, here shown in the east elevation and a schematic view of the chambers, is considered the most refined and probably the last achievement of the Mayas at Uxmal. This building is a composite of a number of Puuc architectural elements brought together to make up an edifice of harmony and repose.

The mosaic façades of the buildings at Uxmal, such as on the House of the Governor, were made by fitting separately thousands of elaborately designed and cut stones into the

rubble core of the building. This technique followed the design and decoration of buildings at Mitla, near Oxaca in south-central Mexico, an area where the art was even more refined.

Generally speaking, the architecture at Uxmal is Puuc-Maya and falls into the Florescent period of Classic Maya development. It was strongly influenced by non-Maya techniques, for during the final centuries of the Classic Mayas there was a struggle for the domination of all of Yucatán directly or indirectly by groups from the Valley of Mexico. These peoples, who brought about the incursion of foreigners into Yucatán, finally allied themselves together and located in Chichén Itzá in about A.D. 800. We do not know exactly what their relationship with the Puuc area was beyond the fact that evidence of the non-Maya influence is found in the architecture of Uxmal and the surrounding area.

17

From Proskouriakoff, *An Album of Maya Architecture*

Palace at Sayil

Sayil: This is a Puuc-style storied (or chambered) palace pyramid. The columned doorways are a common feature of the construction in Yucatán, "and their rhythmic alternation with simple rectangular openings is one of the pleasing traits of the Puuc style," all of which combine to make this structure "one of the most satisfactory compositions that the Maya ever created (Proskouriakoff, 1963: 56)."

At Sayil there is a *chultun* located near the northwest corner of the Palace, which was designed and built to store rain water. Puuc area *chultunes* were also used as granaries for the storage of food and seed.

18

From Proskouriakoff, *An Album of Maya Architecture*

Arch at Labná

Labná: The portal arch at Labná is a typical Puuc structure. Ordinarily such an arch is designed as a part of a building in the way that the arches are an integral part of the Palace of the Governor at Uxmal, but in other Puuc areas, such as Kabah, the independent arch serves as a monumental gateway. This arch represents a fusion of the two concepts. It was a part of the palace structure at Labná, yet it stands alone as a complete unit. The roof comb, as Tatiana Proskouriakoff has envisioned it, is somewhat similar to the roof comb of the older building of the Dovecote at Uxmal.

19

There are at least two types of roof combs in Puuc architecture, one with rectangular openings and stucco decoration and the other with perforated stonework frequently in the form of a fret motif. These two types stand side by side at Labná. The arch has rectangular openings and El Mirador has evidence of decorations of stucco.

The roof comb of El Mirador at Labná rises directly over the bearing wall of the front façade and therefore is not strictly speaking a roof comb but rather a flying façade.

On the hut designs which are located on the northeast façade of the Arch are fragments of paint. John L. Stephens reported that there were the traces of color on El Mirador when he first saw it in the 1840's. In fact, most if not all of the Maya buildings were painted (as well as the sculpture which adorned them), but only a few remnants of color are still visible.

Chichén Itzá: The architecture at Chichén Itzá represents that which archaeologists refer to as Puuc-Maya, or Florescent period architecture. Buildings of Puuc-Maya construction are primarily on the south side of the Mérida highway, and the Mayanized-Mexican architecture, or modified florescent, is found primarily on the north side.

The Puuc-Maya architecture of Chichén Itzá and the Puuc area, although constructed in the Classic Maya period, contains strong non-Maya elements. As has been pointed out, the Puuc architectural style of Uxmal, for example, with its simple lower façade and ornate upper façade of stone mosaic is predated by construction at Mitla, where the cut-stone motifs are not only earlier but more refined.

It is now established that there was a struggle during the Classic Maya period for domination of Yucatán by various groups of non-Maya peoples who were probably of Mexican origin. The successful groups settled in Chichén Itzá and were responsible for the modified florescent construction. This construction carried a political thrust in that it seems to exem-

plify the effort on the part of the Mayanized-Mexicans to awe and impress.

The principal group of structures at Chichén does not consist of an acropolis, but rather a broad open plaza with the Castillo in the center. More important, however, in terms of the differentiation between the more traditional forms of Puuc-Maya architecture and the Mayanized-Mexican forms is the colonnade. In Puuc architecture, columns were used to widen doorways which otherwise were restricted in size by the stone lintels, but the column was not regarded as an adequate support for the vault. At Chichén Itzá, the column was used as a structural support enabling architects to span a room with several parallel vaults which permitted circulation inside and

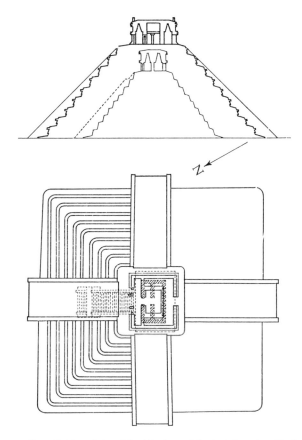

From Kubler, *Art and Architecture of Ancient America*, 2d ed.

Castillo, Chichén Itzá, Cross-section and Floor Plan

From Proskouriakoff, *An Album of Maya Architecture*

Great Plaza, Chichén Itzá

provided lighting from the colonnaded façade. The wooden lintel was used to create a spacious enclosed area. This practice fundamentally changed the concept of the architecture from outward looking to inwardly functional.

The Group of the Thousand Columns exemplifies the innovation; the north building joins the terrace of the Temple of the Warriors and consists of five parallel vaults supported in the interior by round columns. The Mercado, which consists of a long front gallery and a small court in the rear surrounded by a portico, is a further example of Mexican construction.

21

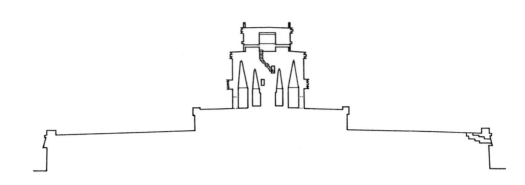

Caracol, Chichén Itzá, Cross-section and Floor Plan

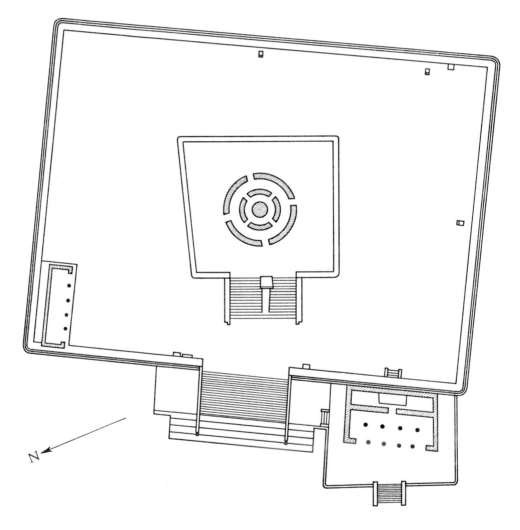

N

From Kubler, *Art and Architecture of Ancient America*, 2d ed.

The Castillo covers a substructure which was a much smaller pyramid and, like most pyramidal platforms of the Classic era, had only one stairway. The profile of the inner structure resembles the architecture of the Puuc. The visible Castillo is Maya-Mexican in style.

The Caracol is a unique example of the cult of Quetzalcoatl (Kukulcán). Its cylindrical form with side-by-side annular vaults and a winding stair in the upper story "may represent the conch shell which was one of the attributes of Quetzalcoatl in his aspect as wind god (Kubler, 1975: 188)."

The sweat house was a common feature of Maya construction. It was possibly used in connection with the ball games and as a result had ritual as well as therapeutic purposes.

All the buildings of both the Florescent and the modified Florescent period were painted. They were thinly stuccoed and then decorated; red was the most common color because it was easiest to produce, but white, blue, black, and yellow were also used. All the paints were mineral based and therefore inorganic, except black, which was produced from burned bone. The color has all but disappeared.

The buildings on the south side of the highway were, except for the Osario, originally of Puuc-Maya style and were later modified by the Mayanized-Mexicans.

The Puuc (or Florescent) style of architecture found at Uxmal and Chichén Itzá during the Classic Maya era contains many non-Maya elements. As has been pointed out, the style employing the simple lower façade and more ornate upper façade of stone mosaic can be found at Mitla, constructed at an earlier date and with more skill. Elements of the Mitla style can also be recognized at Palenque and Seibal. This technique varies from the Classic Maya construction and suggests outside influence in the Puuc area during the Classic Maya period.

Recent evidence indicates an ebb and flow of military activity throughout the Maya lowlands during the last centuries of the Flores-cent period. The murals of Chichén Itzá reveal that there were military incursions by the northern lowland Mayas (from the Yucatán area) into the southern area at Seibal and the Pasión River drainage area. Seibal has many carved monuments, "and these monuments describe a historical succession of leaders, one group from the Northern Maya Lowlands and another group from the area of Palenque, which are referred to as the 'Putun.' These groups are identified by costume elements and mural scenes (Miller, 1976: personal communication)." This indicates that during the Puuc period there was military conflict which is thought to have resulted from the competition for economic advantage in the southern Maya lowlands. In addition, there is recent evidence of fighting between Mayas and non-Maya groups on the east coast of Yucatán at the end of the Classic period and the beginning of the Post-Classic. This military activity was precipitated by the struggle for the control of the land and trade routes of eastern Yucatán.

Modified Florescent Chichén Itzá represents a coalescence of factions following the long periods of internecine warfare among the commercial elements of the Mexican and Maya civilization in Yucatán. The participants may not have been Mexicans in all cases, but the impetus came from highland Mexico. During the turmoil of the end of the Puuc period (about A.D. 800), several of the groups competing for power in Yucatán became dominant, and it is they who settled in Chichén Itzá. They were called the "Itzá" (Miller, 1976: personal communication).

The Itzás were in control, but they were probably insecure as is evidenced by the fact that they felt it necessary to display their power by the construction of grandiose structures that exaggerated militarism and emphasized warriors, warrior cults, and death. This they probably felt to be necessary because of their long struggle to obtain power and because they were foreigners. "Itzá" means "foreigner" or "someone who speaks the language poorly."

There is at Chichén Itzá a common architectural element found all over Yucatán: the Puuc style. But at Chichén there is a unique element, the modified Florescent architecture, found nowhere else. The modified Florescent is embodied in the construction on the north side of the highway at Chichén and appears in the exaggerated emphasis placed on size, scale, and militarism and the highland Mexico techniques.

The Itzás were obsessed with human sacrifice and blood-letting, and displayed such elements on their architecture for the political purpose of impressing their subjects and enemies in order to retain political control.

In summary, we can say that the Itzás were Mayanized-Mexicans who were an amalgamation of the groups of Maya and Mexican peoples that finally obtained hegemony over Yucatán in culmination of several hundreds of years of struggle; that they were insecure in this position and evidenced their insecurity in their architecture and art, which was massive and sanguinary; and that, despite their efforts to maintain power, they were overthrown. Chichén Itzá was abandoned by about A.D. 1200.

Tulum: On the east coast of Yucatán and at Tulum the most distinctive characteristic of the architecture of the Mayas as compared with the rest of the Yucatán peninsula was the use of flat ceilings supported by beams rather than a vault. The ceilings were constructed in the palaces at Tulum in characteristic east coast style by the utilization of large wooden beams on which small poles of two or three inches in diameter were laid. The poles were then covered with a foot or more of cement and rubble. This architectural device made much larger rooms possible with more interior lighting.

With this brief introduction to the Mayas, their history, and their culture, we are now ready to look at some of their achievements—which words alone cannot describe.

24

Palenque

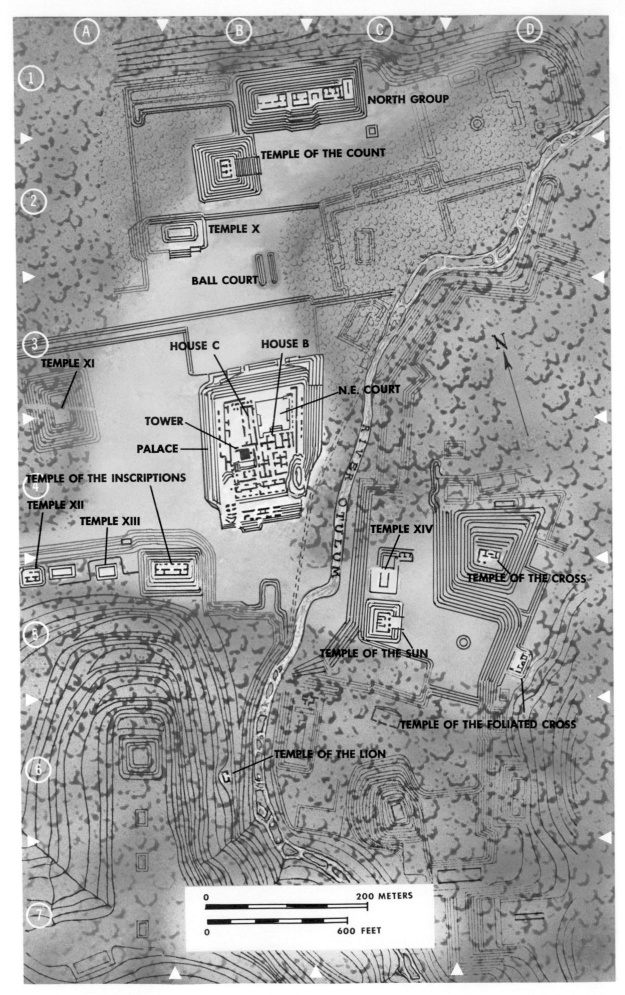

A   B   C   D

1

NORTH GROUP

TEMPLE OF THE COUNT

2

TEMPLE X

BALL COURT

3

TEMPLE XI

HOUSE C   HOUSE B

N.E. COURT

TOWER

PALACE

TEMPLE OF THE INSCRIPTIONS

4

TEMPLE XII

TEMPLE XIII

TEMPLE XIV

TEMPLE OF THE CROSS

5

TEMPLE OF THE SUN

TEMPLE OF THE FOLIATED CROSS

TEMPLE OF THE LION

6

N

RIVER OTULUM

0   200 METERS

0   600 FEET

7

Palenque

Palenque

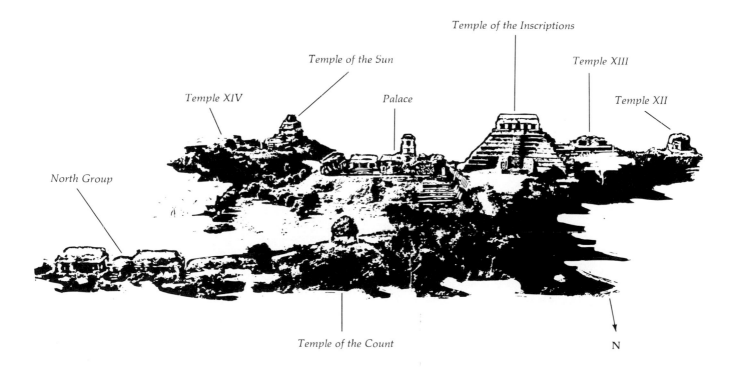

North Group

Temple XIV

Temple of the Sun

Palace

Temple of the Inscriptions

Temple XIII

Temple XII

Temple of the Count

N

27

Magnificent Palenque is set like a jewel on a natural platform in the forest on the north slope of the Sierra de Chiapas. The ruins sit two hundred feet above the plain that stretches some fifty miles north to the Gulf of Mexico.

The excavated ruins are bounded on the north by an escarpment and on the south by spurs of the sierra. Only a small portion of the city has been excavated. The area you see here is no more than five hundred yards from east to west (left to right) and three hundred yards from north to south. Unexcavated buildings are found from the foot of the hills to several hundred feet above the excavated buildings, and isolated groups of unexcavated buildings extend some five to seven miles east to west.

In recent years Maya scholars, particularly Linda Schele, Peter Mathews, Floyd Lounsbury, David Kelley, Robert Rands and Merle Green Robertson, have made preliminary breakthroughs in understanding the inscriptions and have constructed a genealogy of the kings of Palenque. The latter covers a period of nearly three hundred years from the accession of Chaacal I in A.D. 501 to the death of Kuk in 783.

Between 9.10.0.0.0 (A.D. 633) and 9.13.0.0.0 (A.D. 692), Palenque suddenly developed from a very minor site to a principal Maya ceremonial center of the west. This period falls within the reigns of Lord Shield Pacal (A.D. 615 to 683) and of his son, Chan-Bahlum (A.D. 683 to 701). Generally speaking, Palenque flowered in the Classic period of Maya culture, which extended from A.D. 600 to 800. Its sculpture and architecture exhibit a unique, local style of great beauty and technical achievement which is remarkable even in the context of the noteworthy arts of the Maya Classic period.

The dominant structures are the Palace with its unique tower and the Temple of the Inscriptions. The Temple of the Inscriptions (A.D. 692) is the more famous because the Egyptian-like tomb of Pacal is located beneath it.

Other temples, with surviving inscriptions, appear to celebrate the accessions and subsequent events in the lives of Palencano rulers. Many of them may contain tombs similar to Lord Shield Pacal's. Linda Schele has speculated that Chan-Bahlum is interred beneath the Temple of the Cross; Lord Hok, who died about A.D. 719, lies beneath Temple XI; and either Pacal's father or his mother is buried beneath the Temple of the Count.

The latest dated object which has been found at Palenque bears the inscription 9.18.9.4.4 (A.D. 799). By this time the flower of Palenque had almost withered. There was no known construction after A.D. 800, trade was languishing, and Palenque's influence had waned.

By A.D. 820, Palenque was abandoned after a life of at least four hundred years.

The Palenque text material was prepared in consultation with Linda Schele, Associate Professor of Art History in the University of South Alabama. She is a member of a team of researchers including David Kelley, Floyd Lounsbury, Peter Mathews, Robert Rands, and Merle Greene Robertson, who have been are are now in the process of collecting, assimilating, and co-ordinating information on Palenque which has come from research in archaeology, iconography, architectural analysis, and epigraphy.

Temple XII

The first structure on the right of the path leading into the ruins of Palenque is Temple XII. It is on the slope of the mountain to the right with its back to the Chiapas rain forest.

No glyphic information is yet available, so estimates of the time of construction must be based on the masonry techniques. It is believed that this temple and Temple XIII, the platform of which can be seen directly to the south, may have been constructed between A.D. 731 and 764. This much is known: A fill was made on the west side of the Temple of the Inscriptions upon which Temples XII and XIII were constructed. Since the fill contains ceramics from the time of Hok (A.D. 701 to 719), it may be assumed that these temples were later than his reign.

Palenque was the northwest outpost between the Maya and non-Maya peoples and was located along the land route between Mexico and Yucatán. There is only a narrow strip of passable terrain, approximately ten to fifteen miles wide, between Palenque and the swamp to the north. Any migrations by land to Yucatán had, because of the nature of the terrain, to pass near Palenque. Whatever the causes—externally by the Mexicans or internally by virtue of loss of trade, labor, or food supply—Palenque was substantially finished by A.D. 800, a year important in the rise of Christian Europe, for in that year, in Rome, Charlemagne was crowned Emperor of the Holy Roman Empire.

Temple XII

Temple of the Inscriptions (Palenque)

Temple of the Inscriptions

On the platform at the summit of a stepped pyramid is the Temple of the Inscriptions, so called because of the panels of glyphs just inside the center entrance. In 1952, Alberto Ruz L'Huillier discovered a funerary crypt in the base of the pyramid, the tomb of Lord Shield Pacal, who ruled Palenque from A.D. 615 to 683. Construction of the Temple of the Inscriptions was probably begun in 9.12.0.0.0 (A.D. 672 ± 5 years) and was not finished until after 9.12.10.0.0 (A.D. 682).

The pyramid is some seventy-five feet high, and it was, according to Ruz, who supervised the excavation and reconstruction, revamped twice in later periods. What you see here represents the first phase with eight stepped terraces. The narrow stairway at the upper level, with no ramps or *alfardas*, originally extended from ground level. Later the pyramid was modified by the addition of a wider flight of stairs, the remains of which can be seen at the lower level. It faces to the north and is connected in the rear to the northern flank of the Sierra de Chiapas. The roof was originally capped with a comb and was decorated with stucco figures.

Inside the temple are three tablets of glyphs. The east tablet records the ancestral history of the rulers of Palenque, beginning with the accession of Chaacal I about A.D. 500 and end-

Temple of the Inscriptions (northeast view)

ing with the accession of Pacal in 615. The middle tablet juxtaposes Pacal with various deities in celebration of four katuns of Pacal's life—A.D. 613, 623, 643, and 663. In accord with the philosophical Maya concept of the cycles of time, the text of the third tablet associates Pacal's accession with a similar event which occurred 2,838,844 years, 109 days in the past. The same text celebrates the anniversary of his accession 2,930 years, 146 days in the future. The tablets also record the marriage and/or accession and death of Pacal's wife, Pacal's death and the accession of his son, Chan-Bahlum, to the throne of Palenque 132 days after the death of his father.

The east and west portions of the substruc-ture have been recently restored. There are five portals leading into the building. The four center piers exhibit the remains of stucco figures, each holding a child in the guise of the deity known as God K.

The rear gallery of the temple is subdivided into three chambers. An opening in the floor of the center chamber leads to a steep flight of stairs down into the core of the pyramid to the crypt of Pacal. The stairway was filled with rubble and sealed at the top with stone slabs. One of the slabs has a double row of holes, each of which had stone stoppers. The vault and stairway were discovered after Ruz found, in 1949, that the walls of the temple did not end at floor level but went deeper

31

From Morley and Brainerd, *The Ancient Maya*

Temple of the Inscriptions, showing stairway and crypt

down, suggesting that there was some sort of structure under the floor. Excavation led to the discovery of the vault and later of the rubble-filled stairway into the crypt.

Several years were required to clear out the rubble, after which, Ruz writes, "When the exploration reached the foot of the stairs, we discovered a passage which was sealed with a solid masonry fill. A cist for offerings was found in front of the fill containing clay dishes, shells full of red pigment, jade earplugs, and beads and a pearl." The skeletons of six sacrificial victims were found in the compartment just outside the crypt.

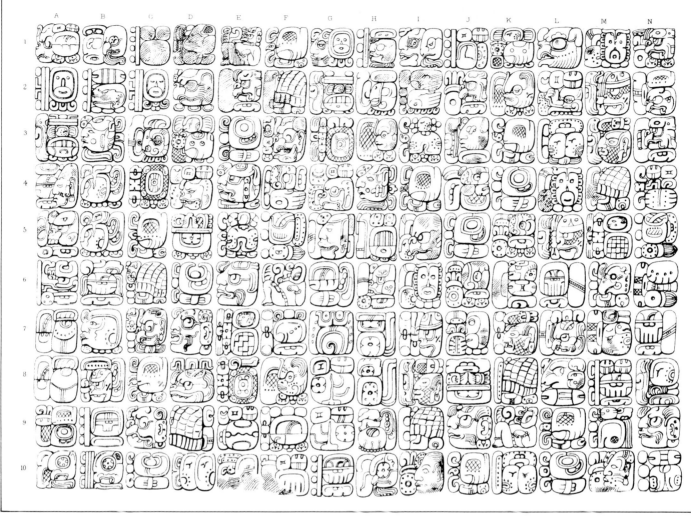

From A. P. Maudslay, *Biologia Centrali Americana: Archaeology, IV*

Center Tablet, Temple of the Inscriptions

This tablet of glyphs was made in celebration of the eleventh and twelfth katun endings in the life of Pacal the Great. Here Pacal is associated with three gods: God L, God K, and the Jaguar God of the underworld. These three deities are considered the Palenque triad.

Sepulchre Slab

Photograph by Merle Greene Robertson

Crypt—Sepulchre Slab

Inside the crypt, down the stone stairway some eighty feet below the Temple of the Inscriptions, is the sepulchre containing the remains of Lord Shield Pacal, the king of Palenque who brought his city to greatness before his death in A.D. 683. The vault was covered with a flat, twelve-foot, five-ton stone lid decorated with the semireclining figure of Pacal and a schema of the cosmos as the Palencanos envisioned it.

The magnificently incised slab represents Pacal in death. Behind him is a cross representing the branches of the sacred ceiba tree—with its roots in the underworld, trunk in the world, and branches in the upper world where sits a serpent-bird. In the branches also is a bicephalic serpent.

The tomb is divided into three sculptural areas composed of the sepulchral slab, the side walls of the sarcophagus, and the walls of the tomb. From the glyphs and figures in this tomb, much of the history and progression of rulers of Palenque have been deciphered.

Pacal is represented at the instant of death, falling toward the earth monster. His head is pierced by the symbols of God K, the deity of kingship and royal authority. God K is depicted, with his flared forehead and serpent foot, on the walls of the tomb and on the sarcophagus lid. He appears as the small figure emerging from the jaws of the serpent just above the knee of Pacal. The serpent-bird at the top of the cross has a shell sign attached to its forehead and a sun-Ahau sign attached to its tail.

The slab is an allegory of the death and rebirth of Lord Pacal. He is represented as falling with the setting sun into the skeletal jaws of the monster of the underworld in the same manner in which the Mayas considered the sun to enter the underworld at the end of each day. It is more than an allegory, however, because the Temple of the Inscriptions itself is so constructed that on the day of the winter solstice the sun actually appears to sink into Pacal's tomb. The slab, therefore, in addition to being a mythological representation of the death of the sun and of the king, is a representation of the cosmological event of day and night and the motion of the sun, as it appears from the earth, during the year.

Pacal rests on the Maya symbols representing death. The shell to the left represents the underworld, and the symbol to the right is that of death. The stingray spine in the center is the symbol of sacrifice and bloodletting. The sun is represented immediately below the figure of Pacal as a half-fleshed, half-skeletal monster, which symbolizes the setting of the sun and the act of dying. The celestial bird is possibly present as a witness for the gods. This is a part of the symbolism which is involved in the concept that Pacal, a living deity, becomes in death a god in the other world.

Palace and Temple of the Inscriptions

Palace Group

This is a ground view looking south from the North Group. In the center is the Palace, showing the remains of the north stairway. A portion of House AD still stands at the northwest corner of the Palace; back of that the north end of House C and the Tower are visible. To the left of the Tower is the north façade of House B, which overlooks the famous northeast court. At the extreme left is a portion of House A.

To the right (west) is the great Temple of the Inscriptions, which has been restored by Ruz as it was in the early phase except for the lower steps, which are a limited representation of a later phase of remodeling.

To the extreme right are the remains of Temple XIII.

Palace (Palenque)

The Palace

The Palace at Palenque is one of the most unusual structures built by the Classic Mayas. The building complex is situated on a rectangular artificial fill and is roughly the size of an American city block (300 feet by 240 feet), with a four-storied tower, glyph-lined courts, and decorated galleries overlaying a labyrinth of underground passageways. The two outstanding features of the Palace are the Tower, which is unique in Maya architecture, and the Northeast Court with its life-sized sculptures and hieroglyphic stairway.

All of the buildings are in the Palencano style, with inward leaning, corbelled walls. The roofs (except for House E) originally bore roof combs. The impressive west approach steps have only recently been excavated, as have the underground galleries in the south portion of the complex.

The Palace appears to have been an administrative center, not a place of residence. It has been suggested that the activities which took place in the Palace of Palenque were probably similar to those depicted by the murals of Bonampak which have been reproduced in the Mexican National Museum of Anthropology and many other places in Mexico. It was a place where the executive and judicial functions of government were conducted, but it is unlikely that the royal family actually lived in the Palace.

The visible portion of the Palace was built over a period of more than 120 years from about A.D. 650, when the *subterraneos* at the

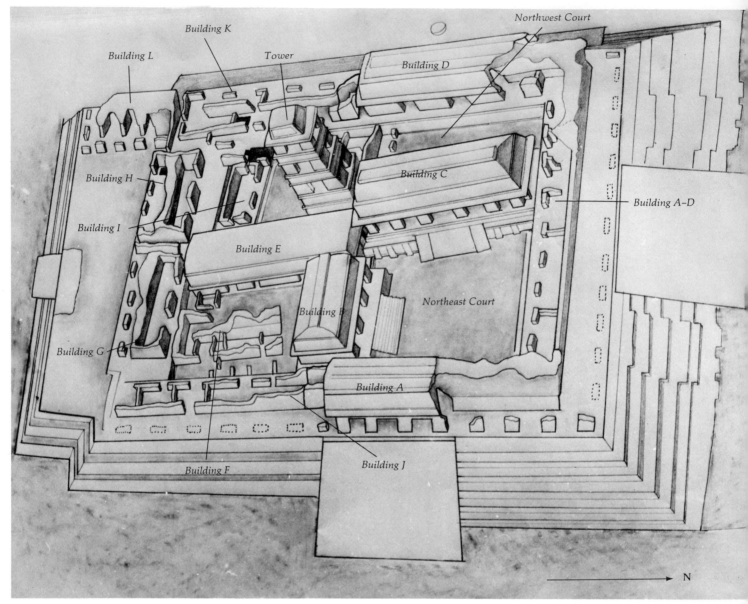

Building L   Building K   Tower   Northwest Court   Building D   Building C   Building A–D   Northeast Court   Building H   Building I   Building E   Building B   Building G   Building A   Building F   Building J   N

Drawing by Linda Schele

Palace Plan

south end of the complex were constructed, to about A.D. 770, when Houses F, G, H, and I were added to the south portion of the complex.

Pacal the Great built House C, which now overlooks the northeast and northwest courts, and Houses B, E, J, and K, all of which comprise the now central area of the Palace. Lord Hok, second son of Pacal, made the grandiose additions to the north portion of the Palace by adding Houses A, AD, and D, and the most obvious addition, the Tower. The other buildings were added later by subsequent rulers, particularly in the period of Palenque's decline by Lord Kuk after his accession in A.D. 764.

The Palace was designed with urinals and a steam bath and was so constructed that the private areas used by the royal family were screened from the public areas.

Palace (west steps and Building D)

Palace—West Steps and Building D

The west stairway of the Palace was excavated by Acosta in the middle and late 1960's. This portion of the Palace exhibits two or more periods of construction. The overlay of later construction periods can be clearly seen on either side of the stairway. Each time the Palace was altered, it was not merely added to but rather renovated to reflect a logical synthesis of change. Building K on the southwest corner of the Palace platform was built by Pacal, but it is now in ruins. The standing portion of the building at the top of the steps (House D) was constructed by Lord Hok as part of the House A, AD, and D complex. House D is a bifaced building with a portico on the west with its stucco-decorated piers and an opening on the east facing the northwest court. The two buildings were carefully linked by a short splice which presented a continuous, integrated façade to the viewer.

Palace Stucco Relief Figure (Building D, pier c)

From A. P. Maudslay, *Biologia Centrali Americana: Archaeology, IV*

Figure (House D, pier c)

The inner, east side of House D had no sculpture or painting, but each outer pier was decorated with stucco reliefs. The bending figure from House D, pier *c*, possibly represents an accession rite; the dancing figure on the left of pier *d* depicts Pacal, and the stand-

From A. P. Maudslay, *Biologia Centrali Americana: Archaeology, IV*

Figure (House D, pier d)

ing figure on the right is either Lady Zac-Kuk, his mother, or Lady Ahpo-Hel, his wife. The stucco figures were constructed by first sculpting the naked figure, then adding the clothing. The stucco itself was made from lime acquired by burning limestone.

Palace Stucco Relief Figure (Building D, pier d)

Palace Tower

As has been pointed out, the Tower is unique in Maya architecture although it has been suggested it may have been a model for a structure in Dzibilchaltún. It sits at the southwest corner of House C.

The building has a nearly square base (23 feet by 24½ feet) upon which four stories are constructed. There are four large doorlike openings on each of the three top floors. The stairway begins at the first story rather than at the ground level.

The Tower was built by Hok, second son of Pacal, around 9.14.10.0.0 (A.D. 721 $\pm$ 10 years) at the same time that Houses A, AD, and D were erected. Probably its primary function was to afford Lord Hok and his royal retinue a vantage point to view the winter solstice sunset (December 22), when the sun appears to drop exactly into the Temple of the Inscriptions. The Tower may in part serve as a phenomenological bridge between House C, which records the birth and accession of Pacal, and the Temple of the Inscriptions, which is his tomb.

The metaphysical and cosmological event of the winter solstice could have been witnessed by thousands of Palencanos gathered in the court of the Temple of the Inscriptions and on the western stairway of the Palace. It is also possible that the Tower was used for astronomical observations of the horizon.

Palace Tower

Palace—Oval Tablet

The oval tablet portrays Pacal and his mother, Lady Zac-Kuk. She is presenting a headdress to Pacal, who is seated, cross-legged in Maya fashion, on a bicephalic jaguar throne. Lady Zac-Kuk, or Lady White Quetzal, reigned at Palenque from A.D. 612 until the accession of Pacal in 615. Pacal was only 12 years and 125 days old at the time of his accession, and possibly his mother continued as regent until her death in 640. The glyphs

Oval Tablet of Pacal and Lady Zac-Kuk

above her head represent her name. Next to Pacal, the middle glyph depicts Pacal's name and family shield. The tablet symbolizes and commemorates his accession to power as lord of Palenque.

It is suggested by Merle Greene Robertson that Pacal "may have been required to marry his mother, at least in name. A divine person must marry a divine person." But Pacal is also recorded in a conjectured marriage with Lady Ahpo-Hel. All three recorded sons of Pacal—Chan-Bahlum, Hok, and Xoc—are mentioned as the children of Pacal and Lady Ahpo-Hel. At the present time no known texts record issue from the relationship of Lady Zac-Kuk and Pacal, and in fact the relationship may have been only that of wife inheritance.

Palace Northeast Court (east side)

Palace—Northeast Court (East Side)

On the east side of the Northeast Court flanking the stairway leading to Building A are nine figures—four on the left (north) side of the stairs and five on the right—all more than life-size. The roof to the left has crumbled away, revealing the inner construction.

Each of the figures is carved on a single slab. The slabs have all been cut off at the top to make them even with the top of the basal platform. There is still a debate over whether the figures were carved for their present position or were removed from another building which no longer exists and placed here. The stairway between the figures is origi-

44

nal and has not been reconstructed. The figures may relate to an ancestral ruler or event, and possibly the building was constructed to house the figures. They are thought to have been carved in the early Late Classic period, about A.D. 615 to 625.

Building A, the Northeast Court, the north elevation of the Palace, and Building D were built about 9.14.10.0.0 ($\pm$ 10 years), or A.D. 721, by Hok following his accession. This group of buildings reproduces the concepts of the group of the Cross (Temples of the Cross, Foliated Cross, and Sun) which were dedicated by Chan-Bahlum in 9.13.0.0.0, some thirty years earlier and manifests the continuity of royal authority (see page 52).

Sculptured Figures in Palace Northeast Court

The figure to the extreme right, above, has an enormous circumcised phallus which has been perforated. The loin cloth goes behind the scrotum. The figure is bound, and the pose suggests that he may be a sacrificial victim awaiting his turn. The individual figure (pictured separately) is located on the north side of the stairway. He is kneeling with one arm across the chest and the other on his hip. This gesture is most often identified with subordinate figures in Maya art and appears to designate an act of obeisance or submission. These figures are not necessarily all slaves or captives and may well represent chiefs, but in any event, they are all in a subordinate position.

Palace Northeast Court (west side)

Palace—Northeast Court (west side)

This is a view of Building C, located on the west side of the Northeast Court. The figures on each side of the stairway face the stairs and were probably carved to fit this position. They are kneeling and making gestures of submission. Each figure directs his attention to the hieroglyphic stairway, which sets out the birth and accession dates of Pacal. From this, it may be conjectured that they are all supportive of Pacal. As subordinate figures, they could be ancestors, relatives, or sub-chiefs from the area around Palenque.

Building C and this substructure were constructed or dedicated about 9.11.10.0.0 (A.D. 662) during the reign of Pacal.

The enlarged plaque of four glyphs is on the north side of the glyph stairway and has not been deciphered.

Hieroglyphic Stairway, Palace Northeast Court

Palace—Hieroglyphic Stairway

On the west side of the Northeast Court of the Palace is the famous hieroglyphic stairway. The glyphs (read in columns of two from top to bottom, riser to tread, and left to right) give the dates of the birth of Pacal, 9.8.9.13.0 (A.D. 603) and his accession 9.9.2.4.8 (A.D. 615). The two glyphs on the lower step to the left mean "accession" and "Pacal."

In addition, there are some interesting aspects to this stairway that are not as yet fully deciphered which relate to Shield Jaguar of Yaxchilán showing possible political or dynastic connections between Palenque and Yaxchilán.

In Western culture the fixed point for the computation of time is the birth of Christ. The Maya Long Count calculates from a point in the past denominated 13.0.0.0.0, 4 Ahau 8 Cumhu. The 13 refers to baktuns (144,000 days), the zeros refer to katuns (7,200 days), tuns (360 days), uinals (20 days), and kins (1 day). This fixed date corresponds to August 11, 3114 B.C. (Thompson correlation). The earliest-known Maya date correlates with the year A.D. 291. There is recent evidence, however, that the Long Count calendar was in use at a considerably earlier time.

The enlarged glyph represents nine tuns or nine 360-day years.

Nine Tuns Glyph, Hieroglyphic Stairway

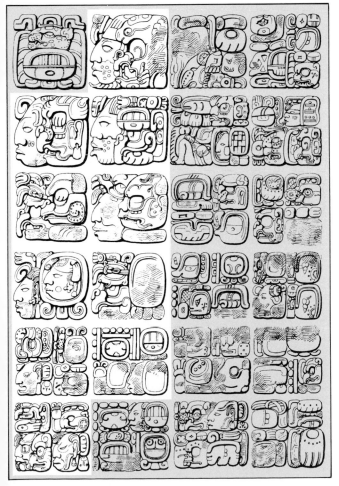

The portion of the stairway which is outlined may be translated "[On] 9.8.9.13.0. 8 Ahau 13 Pop was born Mah Kina Pacal of Palenque, 12.9.8 after the birth, he acceded, Mah Kina 'Screech Owl' Pacal."

Hieroglyphic Stairway

From A. P. Maudslay, *Biologia Centrali Americana: Archaeology, IV*

Palace—Northwest Court and Building C

Palace—Northwest Court

The Northwest Court was constructed about 9.14.10.0.0 (A.D. 721 ± 10 years), some sixty years later than House C to the right. This court was a part of the House A–AD–D construction by Lord Hok. Originally this space was the west face of the pyramid that served as the base of Pacal's House C. The court has no direct outside access and was probably not a place for public ceremonies. Schele speculates that it may have been used only for private royal ceremonies.

House C originally had a frieze decorated with stucco reliefs, and there were reliefs on each of the piers.

The building to the right is House D. Both House C and D are bifaced buildings with openings on the east and west. House C was designed before the enclosure of the Northwest Court, and thus both of its façades repeat the same patterns of piers and doorways. In contrast, House D was designed to present an alternation of sculptured piers and doorways on its western façade, which faced the outside, and to provide small chambers and a dominance of wall surface on its eastern façade, which faced the small Northwest Court. By thus designing primarily toward the function of the spaces to be served by House D rather than toward its internal symmetry helped render the Palace (a structure assembled over a minimum period of two hundred years) a functional, spatial whole, rather than a combination of separate parts.

Palace Throne

Palace Throne

The throne was originally part of a six-tablet display which bears a date of 9.11.0.0.0 (A.D. 662). Pacal's name appears on the throne, as does a representation of the bi-cephalic celestial monster. This is not a commemoration of an accession, but more probably a celebration of a katun ending—possibly the first katun following the death of Pacal's mother.

Drawing by Linda Schele

Panel in Temple of the Cross

Temple of the Cross

The Temple of the Cross, according to Linda Schele, very likely was constructed in celebration of the accession and subsequent events of the life of Chan-Bahlum, who may be buried under it. Pacal, Chan-Bahlum's father, dedicated one structure, the Temple of the Inscriptions, to record his ancestry, his life, and his death and to demonstrate his divinity. Chan-Bahlum constructed three buildings—the Temples of the Cross, Foliated Cross, and the Sun—which repeat the program of texts and pictorial information from the Temple of the Inscriptions. The roof comb of the Temple of the Cross has an internal stairwell which enabled persons to reach a point of observation somewhat higher than the top of the Temple of the Inscriptions. In combination, the works of Pacal and Chan-Bahlum established a permanent record of the history of the Palenque dynasty, their individual right to royal power, the mythological base of royal power, and personal history in both a historical and cosmological context.

The glyph panels which were displayed in

Temple of the Cross

the Temple of the Cross, together with the east panel of glyphs in the Temple of the Inscriptions, furnish the data for the prehistory of Palenque beginning in A.D. 465. The stone tablet, originally found in the rear of the sanctuary of the Temple of the Cross, showing Chan-Bahlum and his father, Lord Shield Pacal, has been removed, but the right panel depicting God L smoking a cigar and the left panel depicting Chan-Bahlum after accession to royal office are still in place.

The façade of the building has collapsed. If you will look back to your left at the Temple of the Sun, you will be able to visualize how the Temple of the Cross looked before the collapse of the south bearing wall. The floor plan of the temple is in the form illustrated. The

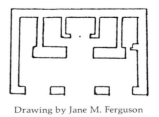

Drawing by Jane M. Ferguson

53

tablet of the cross was located on the back of the inner sanctuary.

The Temple of the Cross faces south and is on the highest pyramidal base of the group of the Cross. All three temples had two galleries formed by parallel corbel vaults perpendicular to the entrance and a cross-vaulted portal in the center wall leading to the inner sanctuary. During the reign of Pacal, the Palencano Mayas developed a unique technical variation on the corbel-vault system used by the Classic Mayas. The two outer corbelled walls are not independently balanced as in other Maya architecture; instead, these two walls lean against the center wall. This structural innovation allowed for thinner bearing walls, more and much wider doors, and the incorporation of a greater volume of internal space. As a result, the interiors of the temples of Palenque are more open, better lighted, and better ventilated than those of other Maya sites. Because the sculptures of Palenque were mounted on the interior walls of the temples, both inscriptional and pictorial information is far more detailed and extensive than at other Maya sites. Plaster sculpture, the major medium of architectural sculpture, became an elaborate and refined art form of great technological and aesthetic achievement.

The Temple of the Cross dominates the interrelated group of these temples. In all three temples, the dead lord, Pacal, is portrayed with the new lord, Chan-Bahlum. All three of the buildings appear to have been dedicated in A.D. 692 during the reign of Chan-Bahlum. This Cross group is an interrelated and highly organized statement of religious and historical conceptions. In only ten years the three temples were designed and constructed, including the great substructure upon which all three pyramidal platforms rest.

Temple of the Foliated Cross

This Temple of the Foliated Cross is similar in construction to the Temple of the Sun, which it faces, except that here the ravages of time have stripped away the front façade. The glyphs indicate that the temple was dedicated in A.D. 692.

The bas-relief is one of the three constructed by Chan-Bahlum to commemorate the transfer of power (in A.D. 684) to him from Pacal. It depicts self-inflicted blood-letting as part of the rites of the cycle of life. The central image and the flanking gods portray life and death. The relief also appears to relate the imagery of accession to the myth of the origin of man from corn.

The Temple of the Foliated Cross sits on the east side of the Cross complex. The central image is the cross which grows from a god-head and is topped by a serpent-bird. The arms of the cross are leafy maize plants with, according to Marvin Cohodas, "the head of the reborn maize deity as the ears of maize (in *Primera Mesa Redonda de Palenque*, II, 95)."

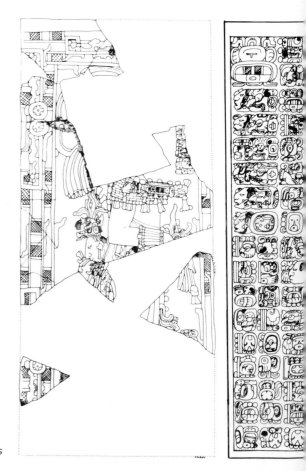

54

Panel from Temple of the Foliated Cross

Temple of the Foliated Cross

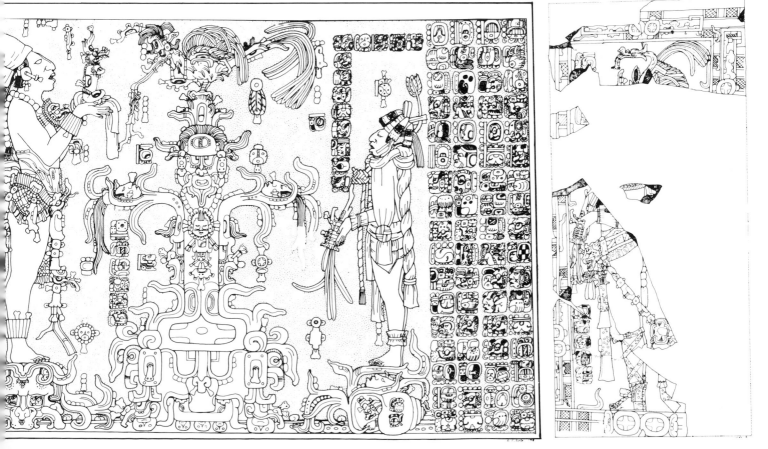

Drawing by Linda Schele

Temple of the Sun

The Temple of the Sun, a graceful, partly excavated, small temple with a well-preserved roof comb, is another of the three exquisite temples which face each other in the southeast corner of the cleared area of Palenque. Finished in A.D. 692, it has three entrances into two galleries, with a shrine in the rear space, and stands on a four-terraced pyramidal base.

This temple with its roof comb is particularly photogenic during the hours of the morning when the light plays on the stucco figures of the roof and pillars, which are themselves silhouetted against the deep green of the Chiapas rain forest. The Temple of the Sun is a "winter temple" since the angle of sunlight in the summer months obscures the detail of the architectural sculpture.

Inside the middle entrance on the wall at the back of the building is a bas-relief. In the center of the panel is a shield representing the sun god in the aspect of the Jaguar God of the Underworld. The Jaguar God is related to war, sacrifice, and the descent of the sun in the west. On each side of the shield, resting upon an altar above two figures that may be underworld gods, are the figures of two lords of the Mayas—Pacal and Chan-Bahlum. Each figure is surrounded by rows of relief glyphs.

To the left is the figure of Pacal—the knotted draperies adorning him may indicate a state of death and perhaps divinity. He is standing on the arched back of an anthropomorphic figure. To the right is his son, Chan-Bahlum. The glyphs above the shield record the date of Chan-Bahlum's inheritance of power and his descent from Pacal and Lady Ahpo-Hel.

The Temple of the Sun is on the west, where, according to Maya cosmology, the sun is swallowed each evening by the earth monster.

Drawing by Linda Schele

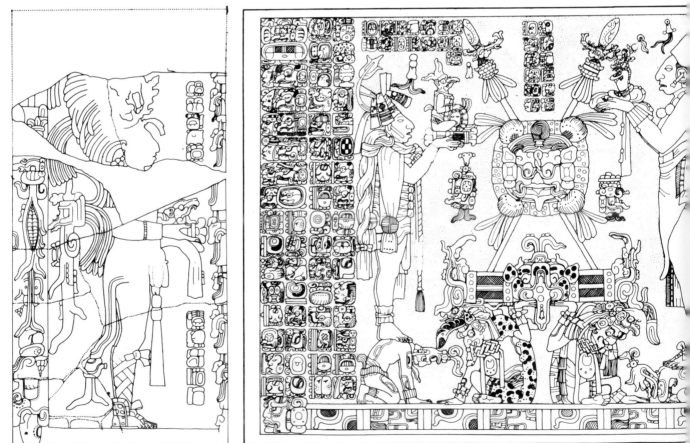

Temple of the Sun, Temple XIV, and Palace

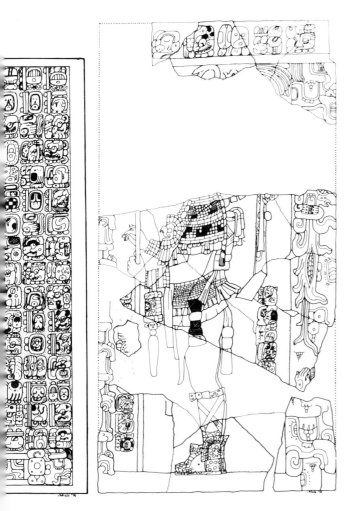

The imagery of the relief of the Temple of the Sun conforms to this symbolism.

Behind the sun god shield are spears with blades protruding from the skeletal mouths of serpents, indicating devouring and death appropriate to the descent and death of the sun.

Temple XIV

Temple XIV is the temple to the right (north) of the Temple of the Sun. It was constructed by Chan Bahlum somewhat later than the complex of the Temples of the Cross, probably about A.D. 697. Its location indicates that it does not fit into the Cross complex and, therefore, was conceived and added later.

57

Panel from Temple of the Sun

Drawing by Linda Schele

Bas-relief in panel from Temple XIV

Temple XIV—Panel

The panel inside depicts Chan Bahlum and
Lady Vulture. He is portrayed dancing, and
she has God K in her hand. The scene may
portray her accession.

Temple of the Count

Temple of the Count

The Temple of the Count is the oldest standing building in the main Palenque area. It was constructed about 9.10.15.0.0 (A.D. 647 ± 5 to 10 years). It is called Temple of the Count because legend says it was occupied for several years by Count Frederic de Waldeck, who explored the ruins in the 1830's.

This temple is a prototype of the Palencano style, with parallel double galleries, the rear one subdivided into three chambers. It was built shortly after the Temple Olvidado was completed about 9.10.14.5.10 (A.D. 646). (The Olvidado is not in the cleared area and is difficult to reach.) These two temples are the first buildings to employ the technique of leaning the outer corbelled upper walls against the center wall. This architectural style is particularly noteworthy because of the mansard effect obtained by the sloping surface of the exterior walls to roughly parallel the inner surface. The sloping surfaces of the vaults are joined to the vertical lower wall by means of a continuous stringcourse which was altered to form a projecting cornice molding. The roof comb over the central axis of the building was designed to enhance the visual height of the structure and may have stabilized the independently balanced center wall.

The Palencano style differs from the Puuc style found in Yucatán in two respects. First, the Palencano upper walls slope inward, roughly following the interior vault; the Yucatán construction, on the other hand, utilizes vertical bearing walls from base to cornice. Second, the Palencano sloping walls above the median molding were decorated with stucco relief elements in the form of figures and masks rather than by stone mosaic decorations as in the Puuc area.

In addition, Palenque structures are often funerary. Under the floor of the entrance of the Temple of the Count were found three graves containing funerary offerings consisting of jade beads, obsidian knives, and shell jewelry. Linda Schele believes that Pacal's father or mother may be buried beneath this temple. She has speculated that the Temple of the Count and the Temple Olvidado were dedicated to Pacal's parents, who both died shortly before the construction of both temples. Because of the lack or the destruction of the hieroglyphic texts from these temples, it is now impossible to determine which temple was dedicated to which parent.

North Group

This is a view of the temples of the North Group looking toward the northeast. The temples face south. Temple III is the small one between Temple II and IV. From left to right are Temples V, IV, and II; all of these structures were constructed after the deaths of Pacal and his son Chan-Bahlum. Temple IV—the center temple—was constructed about 9.13.15.0.0 (A.D. 702 ± 10 years) by Lord Hok, son of Pacal and brother of Chan-Bahlum. Later Hok constructed Temple V (A.D. 707 ± 10 years). These temples were not elab-

orate buildings and were constructed shortly after Hok's accession to power in A.D. 702.

The architecture of these buildings is not substantially different from that of the other buildings of Palenque. The style is Palencano. The front and rear chambers of Temple V have disappeared, leaving only the center bearing wall with three openings and the remains of three chambers in the rear gallery.

Temple IV is also in ruins. Its design was followed by Temple II to the east. Both temples originally had a gallery extending the full length of the building just inside the front piers with three chambers in the rear gallery.

Temple II was constructed by Hok or his son, Chaacal III, in 9.14.10.0.0 (A.D. 721 ± 5 years), ten to twenty years later than Temples IV and V. Chaacal also squeezed the little Temple III (which is pictured on page 62) between II and IV about the same time that he constructed Temple II.

The vaults of Temples IV and V ran east and west and the buildings opened to the south, facing the Palace. These buildings demonstrate the inward lean of the Palencano vault construction. In other Maya construction, at Uxmal for example, any one of the bearing walls may remain standing, but at Palenque the two outside walls never remain standing without the center wall because the outer walls bear structurally on the center wall. This inward lean of the outside wall makes Palencano vault construction the nearest of any Maya architecture to the true arch form.

Temples V, IV, and II

Temples IV and III

Temple III

North Group—Temple III

This small single-vault temple was built in 9.14.10.0.0 (A.D. 721 ± 5 years) and is sandwiched between Temples II and IV. It comprises a single corbel-vault construction; the vault runs perpendicular to the entrance and parallel to the steps.

The technological innovation of inward-leaning walls made possible the wide open spaces in the supporting walls. Door openings can be twice the width of the mass of the supporting wall. Thus these slanting walls enabled the Palencanos to cut out approximately two-thirds of the mass of the bearing wall because the two outside walls leaned against the center wall.

This picture shows the wide opening in the bearing wall made possible by the inward-leaning walls.

Ball Court

Ball Court

The Ball Court—two parallel unexcavated mounds—is one of the oldest known structures at Palenque. It is the only ball court at Palenque and it has been dated A.D. 500 ± 50 years.

Not only is it one of the earliest buildings at Palenque, but it is one of the earliest-known Maya ball courts.

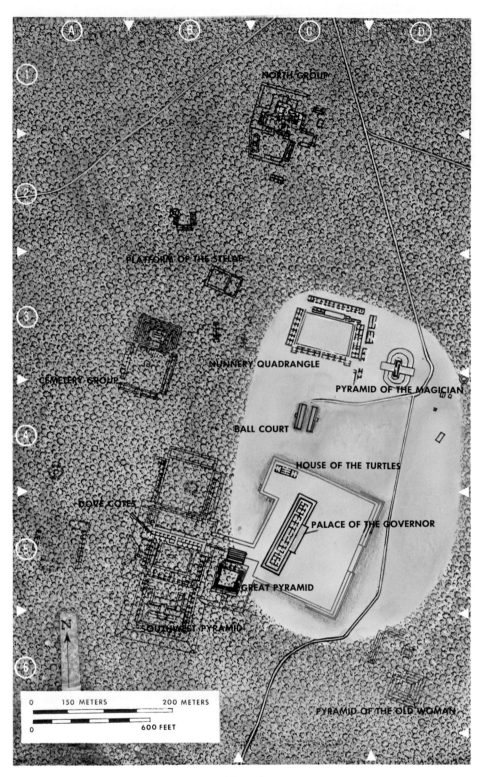

NORTH GROUP

PLATFORM OF THE STELAE

CEMETERY GROUP

NUNNERY QUADRANGLE

PYRAMID OF THE MAGICIAN

BALL COURT

HOUSE OF THE TURTLES

DOVE COTES

PALACE OF THE GOVERNOR

GREAT PYRAMID

SOUTHWEST PYRAMID

N

0   150 METERS   200 METERS

0   600 FEET

PYRAMID OF THE OLD WOMAN

Uxmal

Many Maya cities are found in the Puuc hills of Yucatán, and it is from these hills that their architecture gets its name.

Here is an aerial view of the excavated area of Uxmal looking from south to north. In the left foreground is the Great Pyramid, which is unexcavated on the south side.

To the left of the Great Pyramid are the ruins of the Acropolis with the unexcavated Temple of the Southwest in the lower left foreground. Just to the north of that temple is the Dovecote, which, in reality, is only the standing remnant of the roof comb of the structure—all of the rest of the building has fallen into ruin.

In the center of the picture is the famous Palace of the Governor, which sits atop two platforms. The Palace is considered one of the finest examples of Maya architectural art.

The Uxmal, Kabah, Sayil, Xlapak, and Labná text material was prepared in consultation with Jeff Kowalski of Yale University, author of a forthcoming dissertation on the iconography of Uxmal, and was reviewed by Aruthr G. Miller, Research Associate of the Center for Pre-Columbian Studies, Dumbarton Oaks, Washington, D.C.

Beyond the Governor's Palace plaza, in the middle background, is the Nunnery Quadrangle, a magnificent unit composed of four buildings.

To the right of the Nunnery in the right middle background is the oval pyramid known as the House of the Magician, and directly to the right (east) of it is the entrance to the ruins.

As you look at this beautiful ceremonial center of the Mayas, think of it as a monument to a great civilization that has been dead for almost exactly one thousand years. We are living just past the middle of the twentieth century; this Puuc Maya civilization ended in the middle of the tenth century.

This Maya site complements its natural location. Here, with the arid look of the dry season, the Puuc-style buildings relate to the background of distant hills and the blue of the sky. The Maya architect varied the elevation of each of the structures to please the eyes of his gods and his rulers. Over hundreds of years he created, structure by structure, this magnificent whole, only a small part of which has been excavated for us to see.

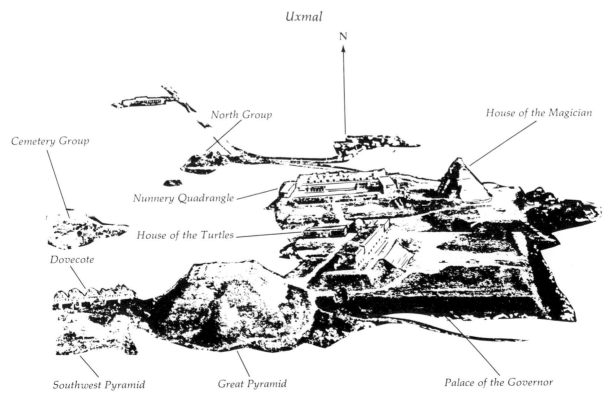

Uxmal

N

Cemetery Group

North Group

House of the Magician

Nunnery Quadrangle

House of the Turtles

Dovecote

Southwest Pyramid

Great Pyramid

Palace of the Governor

Uxmal

Beginning in May and June, the rains come to the Puuc. This is a picture of Yucatán in the middle of June. The bush has turned from brown to deep green. In the background the patches of brown are *milpas*, areas where the bush has been cut for the planting of maize.

Maya slash-and-burn agricultural methods have changed little in more than two thousand years, except that now the bush is cut with a steel machete. The forest is cut in the fall and burned. After the rains come, the maize is planted by dropping seeds into holes made with a sharp stick. From such *milpas* as these

came the two basic staples of the Maya diet: maize and beans.

In this view we are looking toward the northeast and see in the foreground a portion of the governor's Palace and the House of the Turtles.

The north-south axis formed by the Nunnery Quadrangle, the unexcavated ball court, and the House of the Turtles may be seen clearly. The Maya architects of Uxmal created a beautifully organized and interrelated system of outward-looking buildings unsurpassed anywhere in the ancient world.

68

Pyramid of the Magician, Area Entrance (Uxmal)

House of the Magician

The Pyramid of the Magician sits astride the present entrance to the Uxmal ruins. The east façade is faced with a stairway of ninety steps which passes three terraces and reaches a platform which is the setting for the House of the Magician, from which this pyramid and temple take their name. The temple was the last addition to the pyramid and covers portions of four earlier shrines.

The beauty of the House of the Magician springs from its gracefully rounded lines. On the east side the bulk of the pyramid rises in the first unit and diminishes in size three times until the temple is reached. The temple at the summit is the focal point of the structure. The staircase from this view rounds at the edges to complement the pyramid's profile and ascends like a silver curtain from the ground to the temple.

Although the rubble-filled pyramid is faced with limestone blocks which are essentially the same color over all, in the morning light (as here) the color is silver. On the west side in the evening the color changes to gold.

The temple is referred to as the *Casa de Adivino*, Spanish for house of the soothsayer or prophet. The House of the Magician is a rectangular temple containing three rooms

69

and is similar in form to the Palace of the Governor which can be seen to the southwest. The temple is made up of a row of rooms formed by single corbel-vault construction, with the main entrance on the west (which opens into the central chamber) and two openings to the east into the chambers on the north and south.

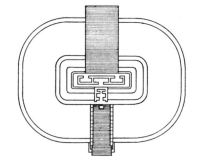

From Kubler, *Art and Architecture of Ancient America*, 2d ed.

Plan, House of the Magician

According to legend, a dwarf, who was hatched from an egg, built this pyramid temple in one night, a feat which inspired the name, House of the Magician.

In the center of the east stairway about three-fourths of the way up there is an opening—made during excavation—which gives entrance to Temple Interior East (Temple II). Inside is a one-room shrine, small and dark, with low round columns and square capitals. This earlier temple was originally reached by a stairway on the east side of the temple which was later covered by the present broad stairway.

Uxmal flowered during the era of the Classic Mayas, who were a people with no metal tools and no usable wheel. This edifice was built by men carrying stone rubble, probably in baskets slung on their backs by a tumpline across the forehead. The rubble was stabilized with cement to form the core of the pyramid and then faced with cut and fitted stone blocks to encase the inner pile. Maya pyramids, therefore, are unlike the more familiar pyramids of Giza in Egypt, formed throughout with fitted blocks of stone.

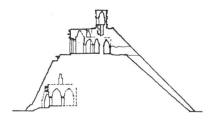

From Kubler, *Art and Architecture of Ancient America*, 2d ed.

Pyramid of the Magician Substructure

In this view of the pyramid, the south end of the original ground-level temple can be seen, which is called the Temple Inferior West (Temple I). Notice that the oval-shaped pyramid was constructed covering Temple I from the east and that the huge stairway on the west extends over it. By entering the opening under the west stairway and looking up, one can see a large stylized mask. This mask is a part of the west façade of the original temple.

At the top of the west stairway, the Chenes Temple can be seen protruding from the west façade of the pyramid. The Chenes Temple plus the ground-level temple and the House of the Magician make three distinct visible temples.

House of the Magician (south view)

House of the Magician (west view)

The west façade of the Pyramid of the Magician is composed of three Maya temples. At the base is the ground-level temple, Temple I, which is also called the Temple Inferior West. It is the oldest temple of the Magician complex and is decorated in the Puuc style. Temple I was constructed by A.D. 600 or perhaps earlier. A lintel showing a radio-carbon date of A.D. 569 has been found in the structure of Temple I.

Superimposed over Temple I is the stairway leading to the Chenes Temple (Temple IV), so called because it follows the architectural tradition of Maya centers of southern Yucatán. The vertical line of the stairway is cut by the stylized masks along the edges. The west façade of this pyramid is characterized by the repetition of stylized masks, which are thought by some scholars to be representations of Chaac, the rain god. Since there were as many as fifty long-nosed Maya deities or phenomena symbols, one cannot state with certainty that these masks specifically represent Chaac.

At the top of the grand stairway is the magnificent entrance to the Chenes Temple. The entrance is the open mouth of a stylized mask. Just above the opening are its nose and eyes. The ears blend into smaller masks (which make up the corners of the temple), and its teeth frame the lintel. The mask portal is a hallmark of the Chenes style. This temple faces away from the additional two stories of the pyramid.

A double stairway was constructed around the Chenes Temple to reach the House of the Magician on the upper level, the third temple visible on the west façade of the pyramid. It was superimposed over Temples II and III, which can no longer be seen, although Temple II can be reached from an opening in the east stairway.

The House of the Magician was built near the end of the Classic Maya period, which extended to at least A.D. 950.

West Stairway Mask, Pyramid of the Magician

West Stairway, Pyramid of the Magician

Here is a closeup view of one of the masks which line the west stairway of the Pyramid of the Magician. The figure is represented with a long, curved snout, spiral-shaped pupils, and square stylized ears from which hang pendants. The band across the forehead probably represents feathers. Below the tubular-shaped decorated cheeks are fangs.

This figure and other similar figures at Uxmal have been identified by some Mayanists as the God B (the rain god), also called Chac or Chaac. It has also been suggested that it may be God K or perhaps an amalgamation of the two. The masks are similar to those found on structure 22 at Copán which bear the glyph symbol for the day Cauac, which is also associated with rain and storms. The similarity of the two, together with some linguistic connections, suggest that this mask may represent Chaac.

On each side of the west stairway extending from ground level to the Chenes Temple is a series of stylized masks, each one above and behind the other. This stairway covered the ground-level temple.

These stairs rise at a very steep (60-degree) angle and the risers on the steps are unusually high. This design may be related to central Mexican architecture. There are many examples of highland Mexican influence in Yucatán architecture. It may be that the steep steps facilitated the practice of human sacrifice. At Tenochtitlán (Mexico City) the Aztecs used the steep steps to facilitate a rapid disposition of the bodies of the sacrificed victims.

73

John L. Stephens in his *Incidents of Travel in Yucatán*, which was first published in 1843, gives a romanticized version of an ancient sacrificial ceremony on the great pyramid as described to him by a local shaman:

Beyond doubt this lofty building was a great Teocalis, "El grande de los Kues," the great temple of idols worshipped by the people of Uxmal, consecrated by their most mysterious rites, the holiest of their holy places. The High Priest had in his Hand a large, broad, and sharp Knife made of Flint. Another Priest carried a wooden collar wrought like a snake. The persons to be sacrificed were conducted one by one up the Steps, stark naked, and as soon as laid on the Stone, had the Collar put upon their Necks, and the four priests took hold of the hands and feet. Then the high Priest with wonderful Dexterity ripped up the Breast, tore out the Heart, reeking, with his Hands, and showed it to the Sun, offering him the Heart and Steam that came from it. Then he turned to the Idol, and threw it in his face, which done, he kicked the body down the steps, and it never stopped till it came to the bottom, because they were very upright.

Chenes Temple, Pyramid of the Magician

Temple of the Magician (Chenes Temple)

The Chenes Temple represents the fourth revamping of the pyramid. It is a cube-shaped tower, busy with masks. It has one portal and two chambers. As has been related, the entrance is the open mouth of a mask, and the entire temple is covered with sculptured mosaics. Superimposed masks compose the corners, with four masks up to the medial molding and three above.

The south elevation of the temple, which can be seen here, has two perpendicular serpents to the right and left of the lattice mosaics which reach up to the medial molding. The serpents are connected to the lower tier of masks. The bodies originate behind the ear plugs and intertwine in a guilloche pattern.

Above the medial molding are six masks divided by what appears to be a series of scrolls.

To the northwest can be seen several unexcavated mounds which constitute the North Group.

Palace of the Governor Complex (Uxmal)

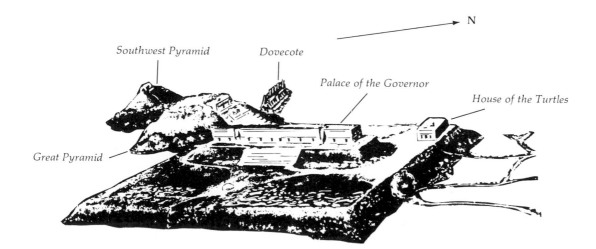

Southwest Pyramid   Dovecote

N

Palace of the Governor

House of the Turtles

Great Pyramid

Palace of the Governor (Uxmal)

Palace of the Governor

This aerial view shows the huge man-made, rubble-filled platform, six hundred by five hundred feet and forty feet high, upon which, in the center, is constructed the Palace of the Governor and on the northwest corner the House of the Turtles. In front of the Palace is an altar which is the platform for the bicephalic jaguar throne, behind which is the *picote*, or whipping post.

To the southwest is the partly excavated and reconstructed Great Pyramid. Beyond that, to the southwest and west, are the remains of the Acropolis with the Dovecote on the north and the Southwest Temple at the opposite end.

The Palace of the Governor and its raised platform covered over an earlier Chenes-Puuc–style building and its plaza, one corner of which can be seen today.

Not only did this great plaza serve as a platform to enhance the beauty of the Palace of the Governor, but also it contributed to the solution of the Puuc Mayas' greatest single problem—water, especially in the dry season.

The Puuc area contains almost no water sources during the six-month dry season. The Mayas were forced to build *chultunes*, or cisterns, into the ceremonial plazas, as here. These *chultunes* filled during the wet season and furnished water when it was dry. It has been estimated that the drainage area of the major plazas of Uxmal could supply five thousand people with water for a full year.

This is a view of the Governor's Palace from the unexcavated pyramid of the Old Woman in the southeast corner of the excavated area. The Palace sits on a huge man-made platform, some 600 feet long and 500 feet wide. Superimposed on the first platform is a second rectangular platform 470 feet long and 23 feet high upon which the magnificent building sits. It has been described as the "most refined and perhaps the last achievement of the architects of Uxmal (Kubler, 1975: 149)." Michael Coe concurs with J. Eric S. Thompson that the Puuc style (of which this building is the epitome) may have lasted until the tenth baktun, 10.8.0.0.0 (A.D. 987), from which we can assume that this building was constructed during the tenth century (Coe, 1966: 109).

Puuc buildings have facings of thin squares of limestone veneer over a cement-and-rubble core. Other Puuc architectural characteristics include: masks, boot-shaped vault stones, decorated cornices, round columns in doorways, half-columns repeated in long rows, stone mosaics on upper façades, and frets and lattice-like designs of criss-crossed elements. Coe comments that the façade of the Governor's Palace is "the finest structure at Uxmal and the culmination of the Puuc style (1966: 109)." He bases this judgment on the magnificent upper façade or frieze, which is covered by an elaborate mosaic of thousands of separate masonry elements set into the rubble core. It is a superb combination of stepped-fret, lattice-work, and mask motifs. The upper façade has been reconstructed by the Mexican government and despite the simplification of the original design, it is impressive.

In the Palace of the Governor there are a double series of parallel rooms. The central chambers are the largest, measuring sixty-two feet in length. There are twenty-four chambers (each vaulted with a corbel arch), eleven doorways on the front and one at each end.

The buildings at Uxmal were named by the Spaniards, who felt that such a building as this must have been occupied by the ruler, and they were probably correct according to the iconography on the frieze. The building is the model for the imposing main structure at the University of Mexico in Mexico City.

This Puuc-style architecture evidences non-Maya influences, possibly from south-central Mexico. Architecture with a plain lower façade and a decorated stone mosaic upper façade is found at Mitla, where the construction is older and more refined than at Uxmal, but the technique is very similar.

Altar

Here is a view of the altar on the east plaza of the Palace of the Governor. In the center of the altar is a throne in the shape of a two-

Altar, Palace of the Governor

headed jaguar. This symbol was important at Uxmal—it is also found on the south side of the north structure of the Nunnery Complex and on Stela 14, where human faces peer from each mouth. It may be noted that Pacal, Lord of Palenque, is pictured on the oval tablet of the Palace at Palenque sitting on a bicephalic jaguar throne similar in form to this one. There, as here, the throne is a symbol of rulership. It also indicates that the House of the Governor is an appropriate name for this building. The throne is cut from a single block of stone 39 inches long and 24 inches high.

This throne was discovered by John L. Stephens, in 1841, who said, "We determined to open [the circular mound]. It was a mere mass of earth and stones; and, on digging down to the depth of three or four feet, a sculptured monument was discovered. It seems intended to represent a double-headed cat or lynx, and is entire with the exception of one foot, which is a little broken. . . . We had it raised to the side of the mound for Mr. Catherwood to draw, and probably it remains there still (1963: 104)."

The low platform in the foreground supported a monolithic column which is larger at the top than the subsurface portion. It has been suggested that this was a phallic symbol; however, Stephens writes that the Indians called this stone the *picote*, or whipping post.

77

Center Entrance Frieze, Palace of the Governor

Frieze Above the Center Entrance

This is a detailed view of the reconstructed frieze above the center entrance on the east elevation of the Palace. The cornice at the top of the building has a negative batter—it slants outward, as does the entire façade of this building. The lower part of the cornice is a boot or S-shaped series of frets representing the serpent which, like a necklace, originally circumscribed the entire building. It has the effect of a straight line interlaced with a serpentine line of identical proportions.

Next below is a line of masks which undulate across the entire frieze. The zig-zag stepped type of pattern of the masks on the frieze is not found on any other building. Usually the masks are in tiers.

The central design is a figure which is prob-ably a portrait of one of the rulers of Uxmal. He wears a headdress of quetzal feathers, and he is placed above emaciated nude figures, evidence of his domination and their submission in the manner of personages on Maya stelae. The figure is flanked by a tiered arrangement of bands, which, if they are continued behind the figure, form bicephalic serpents, suggesting that this is a royal motif or a royal personage. The bicephalic serpent is a typical Maya emblem of rulership. The bands contain glyphs, some of which are astronomical signs. This technique of surrounding and flanking the ruler figure with astronomical glyphs has been found on stelae such as the Ascension stelae at Piedras Negras or Stela I at Quiriguá. The background is composed of detailed lattice-work mosaics and geometric designs.

Arch Detail, Palace of the Governor

Arch Detail

The corbelled arches or vaults in the Palace of the Governor are the tallest of any in Maya construction. Originally they were hallways which provided passage through the building, but were later closed and made into small rooms. Note the vertical tier of five masks on each of the corners where the corbel vault is inset.

Originally there was a series of figures which made up a part of the frieze, but all have disappeared except the one over the center portal.

North Arch, House of the Governor

North Arch

The corbel arch, sometimes referred to as a false arch because it has no keystone, is a hallmark of the Mayas. This one is perhaps the tallest constructed by them.

This is the north arch of the Palace of the Governor. Note the vertical placement of the five masks between the building's medial molding and the cornice on the top. Like the masks on the House of the Magician, the proboscis or nose is the most pronounced feature of this mask, but one can also see its eyes, teeth, ears, and ear pendant—stylized, of course, but still readily recognizable.

This arch had had a portion of the later Maya additions removed, with the result that the vault extended unobstructed from ground level to capstone, some twenty-five feet over all. The north arch, therefore, is now in the form of an open A ($\wedge$) while the south arch is more like a Christmas tree in shape.

Palace of the Governor (west elevation)

West Elevation

The west side of the Governor's Palace faced the Grand Pyramid and the Acropolis complex. There were no doors on this side, and the frieze is not as elaborate as on the east side. The cornice is identical to that on the east side with its negative batter and serpent. The fretwork is also similar to that on the east side, but the masks are in a vertical tier instead of in an undulating series.

House of the Turtles (Uxmal)

Cornice Detail, House of the Turtles

House of the Turtles

The House of the Turtles is located on the northwest corner of the grand terrace of the Governor's Palace. Its calm simplicity compares with the classical temples of ancient Greece. Here we see the eastern face of the building with three portals and an undecorated lower façade up to the medial molding. Above this is a course of colonettes. On the top of the building is a cornice molding set with turtles, from which the temple takes its name.

The colonettes were perhaps placed on the façade of this building to emulate in stone that which had in earlier structures been made of wood. The walls of Maya huts then, as now, were constructed of a series of vertical posts lashed together, and, we may assume, so were the original buildings of wood. Like the Greeks and Egyptians, the Mayas appear to have built of stone that which they originally had built of wood.

Each turtle has a different design, and the turtles are placed at regular intervals along the cornice of the House of the Turtles. Morley and Brainerd quote Bishop Landa as saying that the Mayas "had such a great quantity of

Corbel-Vault Construction,
House of the Turtles

idols, that those of their gods were not enough, for there was not an animal or insect of which they did not make a statue (1963: 221)."

A portion of the south wall and roof has collapsed, and, although partly restored, an opening remains in the roof of the House of the Turtles which reveals the method of construction used by the Puuc Maya. The buildings were in fact a pile of rubble with small cave-like rooms. Morley considers the corbel-vaulted masonry buildings an archaeologically diagnostic characteristic of the Classic Mayas. Here were two corbel-vaulted rooms from which the method of construction can be clearly observed. The arch bore no weight, for it was merely a device for preserving a small open space within a core of cement and rubble.

This corbel-vault construction utilized the technique of moving each higher stone toward the center with a capstone at the top, each stone held in place by the cement and rubble behind it, as can be seen by this cross section of the arch. This technique emulates the construction of the Maya hut, which was built in the same form.

From G. F. Andrews, *Maya Cities*

Corbel Arch Detail, House of the Turtles

The architecture of the Mayas was, like that of the ancient Greeks, to be viewed from the outside.

83

Dovecote (south view)

The Dovecote

This is a view of the Dovecote located at the north portion of the Acropolis as it appears from the unexcavated Southwest Temple (page 86). The building is located to the west of the Great Pyramid and southwest of the Governor's plaza. The building is called the Dovecote because of the original design of the roof comb.

The plan of the Dovecote used a central wall, upon which the comb was constructed, erected on an east-west line. As can be seen, there were vaulted chambers on both the north and south sides of the building. These chambers have collapsed, leaving only the roof combs standing. The roof combs are of open-work design and a triangular motif. A series of chambers were located on each side of the

arched passage and on each side of the building.

The Dovecote is a standing remain of the Acropolis of Uxmal, which was composed of the Great Pyramid to the east and a series of three courtyards of diminishing size ascending from north to south from the Dovecote to the South Pyramid.

George Kubler suggests that this building is typologically older than the free-standing block designs of the Nunnery and Governor's Palace. It may have been constructed in the Middle Classic period some two hundred years before the later construction. This would put the construction probably between A.D. 700 and 800.

The roof comb was originally decorated with low reliefs and figures in stucco.

Great Pyramid and Dovecote

The Great Pyramid

The Great Pyramid has been partly restored. Originally it was terraced with nine levels leading to the first platform, and, as indicated, a stairway was located on the north face.

This pyramid is truncated, with no temple on the top, but did have palace-type buildings around the four sides of the uppermost level. This indicates that the construction is either a midway stage between the typical pyramid and temple and the pyramid-palace construction or that a building was contemplated for the top platform but never completed.

The topmost story contains decorations consistent with the style of Uxmal—masks, frets, mosaic flowers, and crossed bands. The largest of the masks is designed so that the nose forms a step or throne, similar to the Codz-Poop mask at Kabah.

Temple, Southwest Pyramid

This unexcavated temple is located at the south end of a series of three ascending courtyards, surrounded by ruined structures.

In the foreground is a building with a roof designed to form the next higher plaza to the south.

Southwest Acropolis

From Proskouriakoff, *An Album of Maya Architecture*

Ball Court and Nunnery (south view)

Ball Court and Nunnery

The Maya architects, like the ancient Athenians, were masters of outward-looking architecture. Each building and group of buildings relate visually one to another. Here, an observer standing at the north end of the Governor's Palace plaza near the House of the Turtles could look north across the ball court and see all four of the buildings of the Nunnery Quadrangle. The buildings are so arranged that from this vantage point the four seem to be one. The north building—the one in the middle background—sits on an elevated platform (as do the buildings on the east and west) so as to be seen as a unit. In the foreground are two unexcavated parallel mounds which constituted the ball court.

From this point on the plaza of the Governor, the view is spectacular in any direction. Ahead is the ball court, and through it is the Nunnery Quadrangle, with the portal vault giving the quadrangle a feeling of unity. Beyond the arch, the visual effect is heightened by the series of mask towers of the north building serrating the blue sky. To the right of the Nunnery, the great Pyramid of the Magician rises majestically.

*Nunnery Quadrangle
(Uxmal)*

Nunnery Quadrangle

These views, taken from the northeast and west, show the Nunnery Quadrangle. The Nunnery—so named by the Spaniards because of the similarity of the buildings to the monasteries and nunneries of Spain—is the series of four buildings forming a quadrangle to the west of the House of the Magician.

As has been said, the House of the Magician appears to change color according to the position of the sun. In the photograph taken in the morning from the east it looks like polished silver; in the one taken from the west in the afternoon, it appears beige and gold.

To the upper left in the east view is the Dovecote, the extreme north end of the Governor's Palace, and the House of the Turtles. Between the House of the Turtles and the Nunnery are two parallel unexcavated mounds which are the ruins of the ball court.

In the upper center, the sun is striking the east façade of the west temple of the Cemetery Group.

Nunnery Quadrangle (aerial view, west)

89

Nunnery (Stela)

This stela, or incised stone monument, stands in the center of the broad stairway on the north side of the Nunnery Plaza. It is so weatherworn that the glyphs are unreadable.

The Puuc area, including Uxmal, has relatively few stelae in comparison with ruins of the Petén and Honduras. In the bush some 150 yards west of the Nunnery is an unrestored platform with the remains of some fifteen stelae lying as they were found and studied by Sylvanus G. Morley.

One of the characteristics of Maya civilization was the erection of dated stela. In such cities as Tikal, Uaxactún and Copán, dated monuments were regularly erected beginning early in the Classic period and continued nearly to the tenth century, but the system of dated stone monuments was never popular in Uxmal.

Nunnery Stela

90

Nunnery North Building

Nunnery (North Building)

The entire Nunnery quadrangle, also called the Casa de las Monjas, is on a man-made platform. The North Building is probably the oldest. As in all the buildings at Uxmal, the buildings of the Nunnery feature the corbel-vault cement-and-rubble construction. This building, like the others, has a façade of pre-cut stones that have been fitted into mosaic patterns.

The North Building has twenty-six chambers and eleven portals. The façade from the base to the medial molding is without decoration, a feature common to all the buildings in the quadrangle and a characteristic of the Puuc style. Above the first molding the façade has been partly restored and has four mask towers. Two corner towers are standing at the east end of the building.

The structure is built on a twenty-two-foot platform reached from the inner court by a broad stairway. Originally the roof-line silhouette was serrated, toothlike, by the mask towers which extend seventeen feet above the medial molding.

Nunnery Venus Temple

Nunnery (North Building)
Venus Temple

On each side of the stairway on the south approach were two plaza-level buildings. On the left (west) side of the stairway is the Venus Temple, four columns forming a portico and three rooms within the building. This is the only structure at Uxmal with columns. Ruz tells us that the Temple of Venus is so named because a motif in the frieze was supposed to refer to the planet Venus, "although perhaps it is really a simplified mask of the Rain god (Ruz, 1974: 22)."

Mask Tower of Nunnery North Building

Mask Corner, Nunnery North Building

North Building, Mask Tower

The Mask Tower pictured is near the east end of the Nunnery North Building. It comprises a tier of masks fitted one above the other, each with a full jaw (upper and lower teeth), a long hooked nose, stylized eyes, and square ears with ear pendants. A vertical border made up of scroll-like stonework is immediately adjacent to the masks, and outside of that is a mosaic of lattice work. At the top of the tier of masks is a mask which has the characteristics of Tláloc, the rain god of the Valley of Mexico, with ringed eyes and a U-shaped lip bar.

Immediately to the east, making up the southeast corner of the Nunnery North Building, is the mask corner. Note that the building's medial molding is in fact a stone serpent with its head facing the rising sun, mouth open. The serpent's body is simply a straight stone course which makes up the center of the molding. Above the serpent's head are four masks in a familiar stylized form—long nose, fangs, square ears, and ear pendants.

Just to the left of the vertical course, outlining the masks, is an anthropomorphic figure fitted on a geometric design. This little fat dwarfish figure wearing a feather is found in other sites in Yucatán.

This is a detailed view of the south façade of the Nunnery North Building. The inset of stones around the door is common to Puuc architecture. Above the door is a three-part molding which is also a characteristic of Puuc buildings. Resting on the molding is a small niche in the façade which serves as the door of a stone replica of a Maya thatched hut. The thatch is made up of bicephalic stylized serpents, with three heads facing east and three facing west.

Above the top undulating double-headed serpent is another molding composed of colonettes, and above that is a stylized mask. Here the mask is shown with fangs, teeth, earplugs, and feathers above the earplugs.

Hut, Nunnery North Building

Nunnery West Building

Nunnery (West Building)

The West Building is considered the last constructed in the Nunnery quadrangle and has the most magnificent frieze found anywhere in ancient Mesoamerica. It is the rococo of Puuc art.

This beautiful building sits on a raised platform and is reached by steps extending the full length of the building. Between the top step and the building platform is a series of short columns. There are seven portals opening to the east—a main central door with three doors on each side. The façade that reaches to the first molding (just at the top of the doors) is plain square-block construction. The coloring of the limestone in various shades of beige contrasts with the darker figures of the Puuc façade. The medial molding has a head on the northeast and southeast corners of the building in the same manner as the North Building and the Governor's Palace. Between the medial molding and the negative battered cornice at the top of the building is an intricately designed panel which completes an ornate and resplendent example of Puuc façade architecture.

There is a special motif over each door. Over the north and south doors is a Maya hut; over the penultimate doors to the north and south is a vertical column of masks; and over the center portal is a throne and standing on it is an anthropomorphic figure of a turtle with the head of an old man.

Detail, Nunnery West Building

The Nunnery West Building is the epitome of the Maya geometric art form. It is a thousand-year-old mosaic masterpiece. The limestone façade is a composite of geometric and naturalistic sculpture. Beautifully proportioned figures are interspersed with stylized geometric areas.

Here is one of the few feathered serpents at Uxmal. It winds across the stone lattice work and around the stepped frets, and is arranged so that the rattles are entwined with the quetzal-feather motif. The tier of masks directly to the left contrasts straight lines and right angles to the undulating line of the serpent and its feathers. Although the feathered serpent is Toltec and evidences a Mexican influence, as here presented it has more of the Maya characteristics than the heavy serpents of Chichén Itzá.

Next on the right of the serpent's open mouth is a male figure—he is in proportion, although only the shoulders and upper arms

Detail, Nunnery West Building

remain of his upper torso. His lower torso may represent a phallus. Above this figure is a jaguar's head positioned on a lattice-work pattern. To the right is an unadorned Maya hut, complete with layers of stone to represent a thatched roof, above which is a stylized mask.

Over the center portal of the West Building of the Nunnery complex is what is probably the symbol of God N. It has a turtle-shell body and the face of an old man. These are the attributes of the Classic Maya God N. Above him is a large circular stacked feather headdress common in the Puuc area. Similar headdresses are found on two of the stelae at Uxmal.

Next to the north corner tier of masks on the lower portion of a stepped-fret abstract design is the face and arms of a figure wearing a mosaic headdress. Just above him is a flowered motif inset in the lower cornice molding.

Nunnery East Building

Nunnery (East Building)

The Nunnery East Building sits to the west of the House of the Magician. It was the third building constructed in this complex. The building has a stairway which extends its entire length, with a series of short columns at the top of the stairway and just below the platform upon which the building itself is placed.

The lower façade is plain. The medial molding just above the five doorways has a series of short columns. On top of these columns is the serpent course with a head at the north end of the building, and above the medial molding is a relatively austere façade composed of lattice work and an inverted triangle of double-headed serpents.

A molding of short columns makes up the base of the cornice, topped by a negative battered cornice of square-cut stones. The molding represents stone serpents with heads on the ends of the building.

Note how the Chenes Temple and the House of the Magician seem to float above the roof of the East Building of the Nunnery.

The façade of the East Building of the Nunnery is plain and subdued in contrast to the flamboyant frieze of the West Building. The center portal is crowned by a tier of masks which make up the center of the façade, but the masks do not extend through the cornice; instead, there is a repetition of the inverted-V design of serpents.

In the upper center of each of the serpent motifs was a protruding face. Four of them are in place and two are missing. At each end of the façade on the building corners are masks with open mouths and stylized eyes. On this building, as on the North and West buildings, masks border the end of the frieze.

Mask Corner, Nunnery East Building

99

Nunnery South Building

Nunnery (South Building)

The South Building of the Nunnery quadrangle is constructed at plaza level. It was built after the North Building, and was the second building in the group to be constructed.

The archway entrance is on an axis with the ball court. Note the variable spacing of the doorways, which have the widest intervals next to the archway and diminishing intervals toward the corners. Over each door is a stone hut with crossed frets and stone columns as background.

This view demonstrates the visual harmony of all the Uxmal buildings. Over the top of this building on the second visible terrace is the Governor's Palace. On the terrace below is the House of the Turtles. The Great Pyramid, the Southwest Pyramid, and the Dovecote can be seen arrayed from left to right.

Cemetery Temple

Cemetery Temple

This is an unexcavated area to the west of the Nunnery. It was a plaza surrounded by several structures, only one of which has been restored.

The West Temple sits upon a stepped pyramid and has three portals and three chambers. No decorations remain on the façade. There is a low roof comb or crest with ten openings, similar to the design of the Dovecote. The type of construction leads one to believe that this temple was built earlier than the major structures of Uxmal.

Cemetery Altar

Cemetery Altar

The Cemetery area gets its name from the altars (or platforms) which are bordered by low-lying stonework inscribed with glyphs and decorated by a pattern of skulls and crossed bones. Note that the corners of the stone courses have the skull inverted. These are *tzompantlis*, which evidence Mexican influence and death imagery.

The round circles with a small inner circle and a tag on the outer periphery are assumed to be extruded eyeballs, called "death eyes," often found on the collar of the death god.

Temple of the Old Woman (Uxmal)

Temple of Old Woman and Phallic Collection

The Temple of the Old Woman is an unexcavated pyramid southeast of the Governor's Palace. Its primary interest to the tourist is a vantage point from which to photograph the plaza of the Palace of the Governor.

To the left (east side) of the trail, which runs south along the edge of the platform of the plaza of the Governor's Palace (just before reaching the path which goes to the Temple of the Old Woman) is a collection of several phallic stones.

The Temple of the Old Woman is part of the myth of the creation of the House of the Magician. The sorceress who lived here was the adoptive mother of the dwarf who overnight created the House of the Magician. There are a few remains of a wall, a frieze, and a portion of open work which would indicate early construction.

Phallic Collection

Temple of the Phallus

Temple of the Phallus

The Temple of the Phallus can be reached by taking the first path to the southwest in front of the Temple of the Old Woman. The path continues in a southwesterly direction for approximately one-quarter of a mile to the unexcavated temple. The only phallus visible is on the south side of the structure just above the lower molding of the cornice.

The phallus may have served, like a gargoyle, as an outlet for the water falling on the roof. Alberto Ruz L'Huillier says, "It is currently known that there are plentiful representations of the phallus at Uxmal, in the human figures appearing on the friezes of the principal façades of the West Building and rear façade of the North Building of the Nunnery, as also in different places outside the structures. It is probable that the phallus is an alien motif, since it is very rare in Maya art, and it is supposed that it dates to the period of Toltec influences and perhaps proceeds from the Huaxtec area, where it is frequently found. The cult of the phallus formed part of the beliefs of the ancient inhabitants of Mexico, not because of its erotic significance but rather as a symbol of fecundity and connected with the fertility of the soil (1974: 50)."

The Puuc Area: Kabah

Kabah

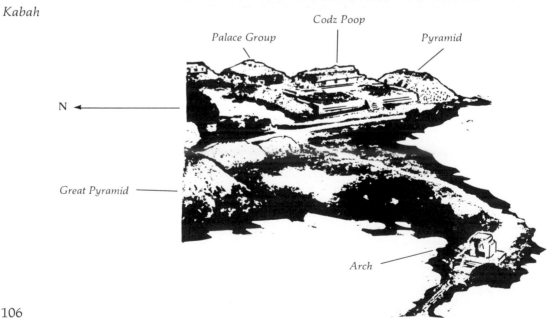

Codz Poop

Palace Group

Pyramid

N

Great Pyramid

Arch

106

Kabah

Kabah is a Puuc center located on Highway 261 south of Uxmal. The highway runs through the ruins with the Codz Poop and the Palace area on the east side of the road and the Great Pyramid and the Arch on the west.

The second aerial view depicts the pyramid which is on the south side of the Codz Poop platform; the Codz Poop and the two buildings to the east make up the Palace group.

It can reasonably be assumed that the Kabah structures you see here were constructed between A.D. 850 and 900 (Miller, 1976: personal communication).

107

Codz Poop (west view)

Codz Poop

The Codz Poop (rolled-up mat) sits on a stepped platform above a large terrace with a stairway on the west. The building is exceptional because of the some 250 masks which cover the entire west front of the building. It is doubtlessly the busiest ancient façade in Yucatán.

The mask decoration begins at platform level rather than at the medial molding, as is usually found in Puuc architecture. The construction is Puuc, but the façade decoration indicates a Chenes influence from the south. The masks are three-tiered both above and below the medial molding, plus a single line below room level. Most of the masks which were originally on the upper façade of the building are gone.

Inside the Codz Poop are two parallel series of five rooms covered by a corbel-vault ceiling constructed on two different levels. The building gets its name from a doorway leading from one of the rooms in the first gallery to one in the second where there is a step formed by a monster mask snout. It has the form of a rolled up rug or mat, hence the name "Codz Poop."

The style is late Classic Puuc. It supports a ten-foot roof comb with rectangular openings of unequal height to produce a serrated or saw-tooth effect against the sky.

Detail, Codz Poop

The façade of the Codz Poop is an overwhelming repetition of stylized masks. The variation in colors (brown, beige, ivory, gray, and black) on the basically gray limestone is the result of the effect of the elements and oxides in the soil that took place while the structure was covered.

The wall is covered with hundreds of eyes staring straight ahead. Between each set of eyes is a greater or lesser trunk going out, down, around, and back. Note that most of the masks' noses have been broken off, but there are still a few masks where the proboscis rolls back in almost a complete circle. The noses serve as steps into the north doors and on the inside of the building.

109

Palace (Kabah)

The Palace

The Palace is a two-story structure with a double-tiered open-work roof comb. The ground floor is forward of the second floor, and its roof constituted the platform in front of the upper building.

This structure has seven west-opening doors, two of which are especially wide and have round columns and square capitals supporting the lintels. Above the medial molding the façade slants inward to the cornice molding producing a mansard-like effect in a construction which appears similar to that of temples at Palenque, but the outside walls do not bear on the central wall as at Palenque.

The decoration consists of a number of small banded colonettes in groups of three spread across the face of the building. Above this part of the façade is a cornice molding consisting of two parallel stone courses with vertically fitted stones between.

Arch (Kabah)

The Arch

The Kabah Arch is an undecorated corbel-vaulted arch constructed on a raised platform with steps leading to the platform. It is assumed to be the gateway to the ceremonial center of Kabah. A *sacbe*, an elevated, paved, ceremonial roadway, leads away from Kabah through this arch in the direction of Uxmal. It may have connected the two sites.

The word *sacbe* (*sacbeob*, plural) means in Maya "white road": *sac* or *zac*, which is "white" and *be*, "road." These roads of limestone vary in height from two to eight feet above the ground level and run in straight lines between building groups. The sides are built of roughly dressed stone, and the tops covered with a natural lime cement called *sahcab*, which hardens under wetting and pressure. The roads are about fifteen feet wide and vary in length from less than one mile to over sixty miles.

The Puuc Area: Sayil

Palace (Sayil)

Sayil is the first stop on the jeep trail which leaves the Campeche-to-Merida highway a few miles south of the Kabah ruins. It sits resplendently and quietly in the Yucatán jungle, the solitude enhancing its beauty. The center level of the Palace has the coloring of a thousand years of weathering. It almost appears as if someone had carefully accented the vertical design with brushed color.

The Palace at Sayil is a part of a site which contains several hundred known structures. It probably dates from about A.D. 850. This complex is the final stage of an evolutionary process which began with a single-story struc-ture with no special features and culminated in this aggregation of structures. "Unfortu-nately," says George Andrews, "it seems to mark the beginning of the end of Maya cre-ativity . . . since Sayil was abandoned not long after the palace was completed (1975: 360)." The guides say Sayil means "place of the ants."

This magnificent building has three stories, each one recessed from the other—the roof of the lowest story provides a terrace for the second, and the second a terrace for the third. Two broad flights of stairs reach the second terrace. The mellow yellow-brown color of

114

Palace

the second-story limestone façade comes from the iron oxide in the soil which covered the palace for centuries.

The ground-floor building has been restored on the east side. The façade is plain up to the medial molding above the doors; above that the frieze is composed of three horizontal tiers of colonettes which reach the cornice. On the west the second story has six openings—two doors and four porticoed chambers, each with two round columns, which, like the classic Greek columns, bulge slightly in the center and are topped by square capitals holding stone lintels. The columns

are smooth, not fluted like their Greek counterparts. Between the porticoes are a series of banded colonettes.

Above the medial molding extending up to the cornice molding is a row of small colonettes broken by a massive mask and a representation of the falling or diving god. At the summit is a rectangular building with doors on the south and on the ends. There is a base molding of colonettes and, so far as one can tell, a plain façade and cornice.

In the aerial view a large *chultun* for storage of water can be seen near the northwest corner of the building.

Palace Mask (Sayil)

The mask is located in the center of the second story west. It is typical of Puuc masks in that it has the following characteristics: curved nose, stylized eyes, ears with pendants, a headdress, and fanglike teeth.

Outbuilding (Sayil)

Outbuilding

One of the many unexcavated structures at Sayil is a small temple located south of the Palace. Its chief interest is its colonette façade, made up of a short course of columns just above the medial molding and a longer course, just above, with center stone spool-shaped bands. The technique of building is clearly visible in the central part of the frieze, where the depressions into which the facing stones were fitted can be seen.

This building demonstrates the destructive force that vegetation can exert on stone buildings given a thousand years of time. The grass and trees have almost, but not quite, claimed this little building for their own. In Yucatán and Quintana Roo there are hundreds, perhaps thousands, of grass-covered mounds hiding buildings ten to fifteen centuries old.

El Mirador (Sayil)

El Mirador

El Mirador is about one-quarter of a mile south of the Palace and is connected with the Palace by a *sacbe*. The temple with its impressive roof comb sits on a platform. It has two rooms and one visible door, which was, however, originally an interior door, for the front of the structure has fallen away.

The protruding stones on the roof comb indicate that the façade of the roof comb was originally decorated with stucco ornamentation, but all that remains is the framework for the decoration except for the pattern of horizontal openings.

Stucco was not common in the Puuc area because of the abundance of limestone, which was used to make stone mosaic decorations. There were, however, some stucco decorations at Sayil, Labná, and Uxmal.

The Puuc Area: Xlapak

Excavated Structure (Xlapak)

While Stephens was at Kabah in the 1840's, he found that "all the ruins scattered about the country are known to the Indians under the general name of 'Xlap-pahk,' which means in Spanish 'paredes viejas,' and in English 'old walls.'" The name, "Xlapak" or "Xlabpak," is now restricted to these ruins located between Sayil and Labná.

Less than ten years ago this building was covered with bush and rubble. In these pictures are two views—from the south and from the east. It is easy to detect the restored portions since the stones are lighter in color and unweathered.

The style is Puuc. The building has a plain lower façade between a double lower and medial molding, each of which has a row of short colonettes between the parallel stone course of each molding. An interesting feature is the engaged column recessed in each corner of the building.

On each corner and over the center portal is a tier of masks. In the area of the upper façade, between the medial molding and the cornice molding, are a set of geometric stepped frets and a curious V-shaped group of seven colonettes, each on a cube-shaped stylobate. The cornice is the same style as the base and medial molding.

Excavated Structure Mask Tower (Xlapak)

These two views of the masks on the building at Xlapak are from the west side of the building and from the southeast corner.

Excavated Structure Mask

The Puuc Area: Labná

Palace from the Plaza (Labná)

The ground-level view of the Labná Palace (El Palacio) is seen here in winter across the wide plaza. The dry season is evidenced by the background of the brown Puuc hills—although the weather is hot and an orange tree stands green in the foreground, the undergrowth of the Puuc jungle is brown and lifeless. To the left is a raised ceremonial paved road, a *sacbe*. The aerial views were taken in June, when the jungle is lush and green. In these pictures the *chultun* built into the second story of the Palace appears as a round white circle. In the aerial photographs the ground-level portion of the building which runs at right angles to the main structure appears to be almost disconnected, as if it were constructed as an afterthought.

The Palace is Puuc style and dates from the end of the Classic period, but is thought to be earlier than the Sayil Palace, which Thompson places about A.D. 850. It is the largest multi-room pyramid in the Puuc area. The terrace

124

Palace (aerial view)

on which the Palace sits is some 550 feet long facing the plaza, and the east-west length of the building is about 440 feet. The top story in its present condition is about 65 feet in height and 350 feet in length.

The first story runs at right angles to the rest of the building (north and south) and its five rooms face east; the second story rambles from west to east and is decorated with masks and representations of the serpent.

The top story has a portico with two columns with square capitals on each. A further feature of this upper level is a round collecting basin connected to a *chultun* located near the center in front of the pair of palace buildings.

George F. Andrews says that since there are at least sixty *chultunes* in the area that can be considered as belonging to Labná proper, a population of three thousand residents may have lived entirely within the confines of the city (G. F. Andrews, 1975: 340),

125

Serpent Detail, Palace (Labná)

Palace Serpent

The human and supernatural heads emerging from the mouth of a serpent or monster is a motif found in Classic Maya art. One can be seen on the frieze of the Nunnery West Building at Uxmal. This kind of iconography is also seen at Chichén Itzá. The mouth appears to be crocodilian, which is believed to give it an affinity with the two-headed monsters which are frequently found at Uxmal.

126

Palace Mask

Part of the frieze above the medial molding is a hook-nosed mask with square stylized ears and ear pendants. A glyph date on the nose of the mask has been interpreted as 10.1.13.0.0 (A.D. 862).

El Mirador and Arch (Labná)

El Mirador

Labná is at the end of a long and difficult jeep drive over holes, boulders, and through clouds of red dust in the dry season and mud holes in the wet season. Anyone is happy to arrive at the simple, uncluttered site.

Labná's special beauty arises in the arrangement of its buildings. El Mirador towers above the site silhouetted by the endless deep blue of the Yucatán sky. The upper half of the façade is darker and appears to have been constructed of stones of diminishing size. Its weathered texture and straight lines against the sky make it majestic and memorable.

This pyramid and temple is called *El Mirador*, Spanish for "observatory" or *El Castillo*, Spanish for "castle." Two platforms have been reconstructed at the top of the pyramid upon which sits the temple.

At the time Stephens visited here in 1841, he observed a stucco relief on the roof comb which he reported displayed a large seated figure in the center with a row of death heads at the top. Traces of bright colors were then still visible. All that now remains of the temple decoration is the lower portion of a tenoned figure located on the southwest corner of the temple.

The protruding stones on the façade of the roof comb formed a base for the stucco relief. Technically, since the roof comb rises directly above the front wall of the structure, it should be called a flying façade. The building faces south, away from the central plaza. One is struck by the singularity of this temple; it appears to be the only temple of any consequence within the main ceremonial area and indicates a sharp break from the traditions of the earlier part of the Classic period when large numbers of temples and temple groups were the order of the day, particularly in the southern area. This gives a further indication that Labná was a minor center, constructed fairly late in the Classic period when the generating force which led to the conceptualization of the temple-oriented ceremonial center was already on the wane (G. F. Andrews, 1975: 344). On this basis we may assume that this area was constructed, as was Sayil, some time after A.D. 850.

Probably Labná was in an area of which Uxmal was the center, for Uxmal was the nucleus of a district which may have covered some one hundred square miles.

El Mirador

Arch (Labná)

Portal Arch

This beautiful and famous Puuc-style arch (more accurately described as a portal vault) led from a small courtyard to El Mirador. It was erected on the south side of the main plaza at the end of a ceremonial way leading from the Palace across the plaza. The gateway was freestanding; the other buildings were probably added later. The view of the east side of the arch shows a geometric design above the medial molding and a well-preserved open-work roof comb. Proskouriakoff in her restoration drawing gives it a roof comb similar to that of the Dovecote at Uxmal.

The most spectacular side of the portal arch is the northeast side, which displays two beautiful thatched Maya huts, one on

Arch (northeast view)

each side of the portal, situated directly above the medial molding. The molding contains an undulating stonework design. On the sides of the huts are stone lattice designs. Note that a mask appears on the arch just above the medial molding, and below it is an engaged (attached) column with a capital. There are still traces of the original paint on the huts.

Originally most, if not all, Maya buildings were thinly stuccoed and then painted.

The southwest side is composed of squares, triangles, and rectangles. The upper façade has been exposed and has darkened accordingly; the lower portion displays the gray and beige colors of walls that have been recently excavated.

East Building (Labná)

East Structure

The East Structure sits on a platform and lies directly east of the Palace. It originally had eight chambers, only five of which are extant. The front façade, which faces west, has an undecorated Puuc-style, lower façade.

Since it has been recently excavated, it displays a patchwork-quilt effect of white, brown, and beige.

The medial molding is composed of two parallel stone courses with small colonettes between and above longer colonettes extending to the cornice.

Chichén Itzá

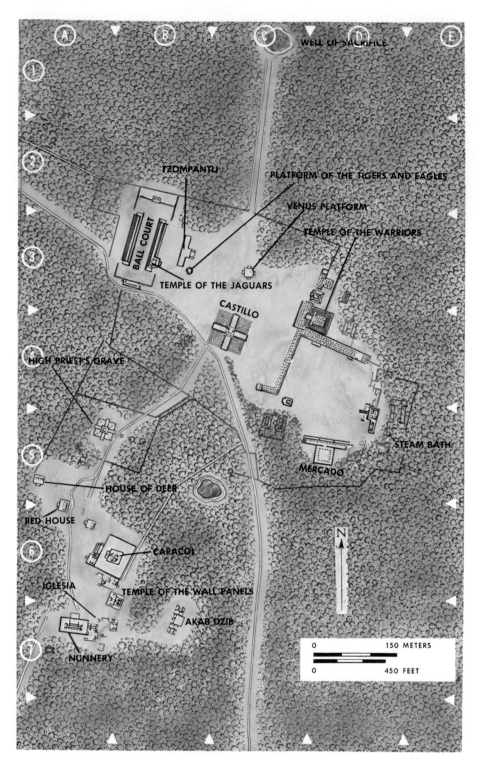

Chichén Itzá

134

Chichén Itzá

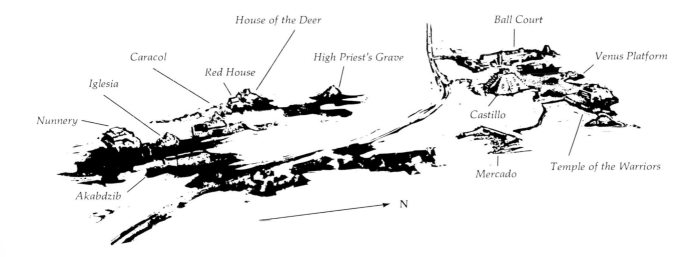

Nunnery

Iglesia

Caracol

Red House

House of the Deer

High Priest's Grave

Ball Court

Venus Platform

Castillo

Temple of the Warriors

Akabdzib

Mercado

N

Chichén Itzá is one of the few Mesoamerican centers whose name has come down to us from the Mayas and was not named by the Spaniards, travelers, or archaeologists. It means "the mouth of the well of the Itzá." The well is the famous sacred cenote of the Mayas. Other names for the site are Uucil-Abnal (seven bushes) or Uucyabnal (seven great owners).

Bishop Landa wrote, "If Yucatán were to gain a name and reputation from the multitude, the grandeur, and the beauty of its buildings, as other regions of the Indies have obtained these by gold, silver, and riches, its glory would have spread like that of Peru and New Spain."

Chichén Itzá is doubtlessly the best known of all Maya ruins. Excavation and restoration was begun in 1923 and continued for twenty years. The site, however, has never been properly studied. The work that has been done is primarily consolidation and restoration, and for this reason definitive dating of the buildings is difficult. Thus, despite the fact that it is well known, it is a site about which the experts know the least. The most promising research in recent years has been the intensive art-historical and ethnohistorical analysis of its famous murals. These murals depict the history of the Itzás, builders of Post-Classic Chichén Itzá (Miller, 1976: personal communication).

This aerial view was taken in March, the season of the year when Yucatán is dry and brown. The green spots are the irrigated areas around the Mayaland and Hacienda hotels. We are looking northwest along the road to Mérida. The village in the distance is Pisté. The highway at the lower left leads to Valladolid and the sea.

In the left-center of the picture, south of the highway, is for the most part that portion of Chichén built originally by the people variously referred to as the "Classic," "Puuc," or "Florescent era" Mayas, between the seventh and tenth centuries. The oldest discovered buildings are datable no earlier than about A.D. 600.

Chichén Itzá was a Classic Maya center, but was not abandoned at the end of the Classic period as were other Maya sites in Yucatán, Guatemala, and Chiapas. In fact, recent research suggests that the founders of Chichén Itzá may have contributed to the social unrest that was one of the major factors that led to the downfall of the Classic Maya civilization in the southern Maya lowlands (Miller, 1976: personal communication). Chichén Itzá's occupation extended into the Post-Classic era. Although there is little reliable archaeological evidence from the site, it is now thought that Chichén was abandoned about A.D. 1200.

The buildings on the north side of the road were all constructed in the Maya Post-Classic period by the Itzás and those you see on the south side, with the exception of the High Priest's Grave, were built in the Classic Maya period and rebuilt later by the Itzás.

At least one of the Mayanized-Mexican periods at Chichén was dominated by the Itzás, who (on the basis of comparative evidence from the Petén) were one of the Mayanized-Mexican groups that struggled for domination of the Yucatán area during the period near 10.3.0.0.0 (A.D. 899) (Miller, 1976: personal communication).

Chichén Itzá represented what may have been the capital for an association of warring groups of invaders who came together here in a kind of uneasy alliance. Arthur Miller suggests that the massive and grandiose architecture indicates the necessity on the part of the rulers to demonstrate dominance during a time of strife and unrest.

The Chichén Itzá text material was prepared in consultation with Arthur G. Miller, Research Associate of the Center for Pre-Columbian Studies, Dumbarton Oaks, Washington, D.C. Dr. Miller is the recipient of the 1976 International Congress of Americanists Award in Archaeology for his study of Chichén Itzá murals. For the past six years he has directed an intensive archaeological project on the east coast of the Yucatán peninsula dedicated to recording and studying the area's rich Maya mural painting tradition in firm archaeological contexts.

J. Eric S. Thompson wrote, "I incline to the idea that the Itzá were Chontal Maya who had come under strong Mexican influence in their homeland at the bottom of the Gulf of Mexico, that they invaded Yucatán, and from the east coast established themselves at Chichén Itzá before the arrival of the feathered serpent cult, possibly in the year A.D. 918. Later, I think, Kukulcán and some followers arrived in Katun 4 Ahau (A.D. 967–87)" and the two groups welded together (Thompson, 1975: 119). *Itzá* means "those of twisted speech," which indicates that they were considered to be outsiders by the native Maya population.

According to recent research, Chichén Itzá was not built and governed by the Toltecs as has been so long believed. It is now known that there was Mexican (non-Maya) influence in Yucatán far earlier than the tenth century—in fact, probably at least two hundred years before the founding of Chichén Itzá, perhaps as early as A.D. 400.

Miller and Fariss have made recent underwater test excavations on the east coast of the Yucatán peninsula at Xelha, near Tulum, and have isolated possible evidence of seaborne invasions of the "Little Descent" people. Much of the low-relief stonework on the Temple of the Warriors at Chichén Itzá is now thought to have been the work of the peoples who made up the "Little Descent" migrations from the east coast, which means that Chichén Itzá was occupied by invaders who were Mayanized-Mexicans rather than Toltecs (Miller, 1976: personal communication).

Michael Coe says the indications are that Chichén Itzá "was abandoned in a Katun 6 Ahau which ended in A.D. 1224 (1966: 128)."

Castillo (Chichén Itzá)

El Castillo

El Castillo is one of the best-known and most imposing Maya structures in Mexico. It was named by Bishop Landa, who was awed by its grandness and reported that it was dedicated to Kukulcán, the feathered serpent.

Beneath the 190-foot-square and 79-foot-high outer temple is a substructure which is slightly smaller. Possibly the outer temple was built on the first fifty-two year cycle after the completion of the inner temple as the Mayas had a penchant for dedicating new structures in thanksgiving to the gods for allowing the world to avoid destruction and continue into the next cycle of time. Although there is no certainty about it, this would place the construction around A.D. 850. The inner structure has nine stages and only one stairway, and was constructed early in the Post-Classic period, perhaps about A.D. 800.

The superimposed temple has four grand stairways which lead to a platform on the top of the pyramid where the temple stands. Two stairways have been restored. There are 91 steps to each stairway, making a total of 364

Castillo

steps, plus one to the top, making a total of 365, which would appear to be related to the number of days in the year. The main entrance to the temple is on the north with two serpent columns and a sanctuary behind. On three sides are vaulted chambers with doorways opening on the east, west, and south.

The pyramid has nine terraces of regularly diminishing size. Each terrace is separated by an undecorated molding. The bodies of serpents with heads on the ground form the *al fardas* of the great stairway to the temple. The façade of the temple is essentially without decoration except for a medial and cornice molding with insets between.

A climb to the temple is a must in order to appreciate the beauty and grandeur of Chichén Itzá. To the north is the *sacbe* which connects the main plaza with the Sacred Cenote or Well of Sacrifice; to the west is the Great Ball Court; to the east is the sprawling Temple of the Warriors with the attached Temple of the Thousand Columns and Mercado; to the south is Classic Maya Chichén.

When the existence of an inner temple was discovered, an excavation was made under

Red Jaguar in Castillo Inner Pyramid

the north stairway of the Castillo to the stairway of the inner pyramid. The excavation continued upward along this stairway to the inner temple, which was completely covered and located immediately beneath the exterior Castillo temple. Here was found the famous Red Jaguar.

On the south side of the upper temple is a hole in the floor equipped with a ladder, so that the tourist may climb down into an excavated hole and see a portion of the south façade of the subtemple of the Castillo. There, protruding from the wall, is a snub-nosed snaggle-toothed jaguar head.

The interior temple can be reached through an opening beneath the north stairway of the Castillo and ascending the stone stairway of the inner pyramid. It consists of two rooms,

the inner room a step above the outer. In the outer room was a chacmool and at the back wall of the inner room was a red-painted jaguar encrusted with jade upon which was a mosaic plaque of turquoise and shell.

The jaguar probably served as a throne for the high priest. Similar thrones can be seen in the low-relief carvings of the lower Temple of the Jaguars across the plaza at the foot of the Great Ball Court. The spots on the coat are represented by inlaid jade disks, the eyes are made of magnificent jade balls, and the fangs are of flint.

The visitor to Chichén Itzá should not fail to make the climb up the narrow stairway inside the Castillo pyramid in order to see this beautiful throne, for it is unusual to find such a *chef d'oeuvre* as this *in situ*.

140

Great Ball Court (Chichén Itzá)

Great Ball Court

The Great Ball Court of Chichén Itzá is the most famous and one of the largest ball courts in Mexico and, in fact, in all Mesoamerica. It is on the west side of the great north plaza. The Temple of the Jaguars rises on the southeast corner, and there are temples at the north and south ends of the court. The outside dimensions are 545 feet by 225 feet, and the field is 480 feet by 120 feet. The target rings are twenty feet above the floor.

The vertical playing faces are unusual as most Maya courts have faces which slant outward. Moreover, the twenty-seven foot walls are much higher than in other courts, as is the goal, which would make scoring substantially more difficult.

This ball court complex was constructed "not long before the Toltec collapse and dispersal . . . that is c.1200 (Kubler, 1975: 196)." The order of construction of the ball-court structures is thought to be as follows:

First: Lower Temple of Jaguars
Second: Parallel playing faces
Third: South and North Temples
Fourth: Upper Temple of Jaguars.

141

Great Ball Court (Chichén Itzá)

This ball court was one of seven constructed in Chichén; six were in use when the city was last occupied. This one is so much larger than those found in Uxmal and Palenque and other Maya sites that it raises the question whether it was designed for the same game. At Chichén the court is nearly the size of a football field as compared with the court at Uxmal which is nearer the size of a tennis court. Since the Chichén Itzá ball court was built later, it may be assumed that the builders knew the size of the courts at older Maya sites. Perhaps this one was built in these grand proportions primarily in order to be ostentatious. The Itzás are thought to have constructed buildings to awe and impress the viewers because they were self-conscious about their position as rulers of, to them, a foreign area (Miller, 1976: personal communication). The Great Ball Court may be an example of this desire.

Great Ball Court Playing Area

Great Ball Court Goal

The Great Ball Court, with a field of play 480 feet by 120 feet and a pair of stone ring goals, constitutes a remarkable construction dedicated to ceremonial play. As has been suggested, this structure is so grandiose by comparison with ball courts found in other Maya ruins that the game may have had a different character. The object of the traditional game was to drive a hard rubber ball through one of the rings. The rules provided that the ball be struck—as in handball or soccer today—by the elbow, wrist, or hip, and these parts of the body were covered with leather pads. A goal was so rare that the winning team won the clothing and jewelry of the spectators.

143

Great Ball Court Bas-Relief

The game had a far more serious side, however, as is shown in the grim panels on each side of the court. Along the bottom of the vertical walls is a low terrace with sloping walls decorated with panels in bas-relief, converging on a central panel, which displays a round ball or shield portraying the head of death, from whose mouth emerges a double-speech glyph. Kneeling on the right of death is the beheaded captain of the losing team with blood in the form of serpents spurting from his neck. On the left stands the winning captain with a flint knife in his right hand and the deceased captain's head in his left.

Temple of the Bearded Man

Temple of the Bearded Man

The graceful temple at the north end of the Ball Court is called the Temple of the Bearded Man; the name is taken from the bas-relief within the sanctuary of the temple. The platform upon which this temple stands is three tiered, and the interior walls are lined with motifs of the earth monster, trees, birds, and flowers.

A portico opens to the south with an entrance between two well-proportioned round columns. This is a beautiful example of post-and-lintel construction.

Tourists are attracted to and intrigued by this temple because of the extraordinary acoustics of the Ball Court. A person speaking in a normal voice at the south end of the court, well beyond the expected range of hearing, can easily be heard in this temple.

145

Detail, Lower Temple of the Jaguars

The lower Temple of the Jaguars in the Ball Court complex was the first structure built in the group. Authorities seem to agree that the construction was contemporaneous with the Castillo, but estimates vary from early to late in the Post-Classic period. The temple was later covered with a pyramid upon which now sits the Temple of the Jaguars with its great serpent columns. The lower temple faces the main plaza; the upper temple overlooks the Ball Court.

A limestone jaguar, looking much like an English bulldog, stands astride the center entrance to the portico of the lower temple and looks menacingly out. He is surrounded by square pillars on which are carved Mayanized-Mexican warriors, lattice work, and monster masks.

Guards, Upper Temple of the Jaguars

From Morley and Brainerd,
The Ancient Maya

*Drawing of Mural in
Temple of Jaguars*

Upper Temple of the Jaguars

The upper Temple of the Jaguars was erected between A.D. 800 and 1050 upon the platform formed by the pyramid constructed over the lower temple at the southeast corner of the Great Ball Court. The temple is reached by a steep course of stairs to the south of the pyramid.

The portico is guarded by two huge serpent columns with heads on the platform and rattles in the air; their bodies form the drums of the column. The heads and bodies are covered with plumes and feathers.

Inside the temple is a wall painting which portrays some Mayanized-Mexicans assaulting other Mayanized-Mexicans. It depicts part of the struggle between invaders for the domination of the area (Miller, 1976: personal communication). It is thought that these battle scenes probably took place about A.D. 890, which is about the time of the end of the Classic Maya period.

147

Venus Platform

Venus Platform (Venus as the morning star)

Venus Platform

On the main plaza to the north of the Castillo is the square Venus Platform, constructed between A.D. 1100 and 1200. It had stairways on four sides and at the top of each stairway *alfarda* was an open-mouthed serpent. The platform is also known as the Tomb of the Chacmool, as a result of the discovery of a chacmool during excavation.

Between the base molding and the cornice is a frieze which portrays Kukulcán and the planet Venus. The symbol is associated with the origin of the Itzás at Chichén which is implicit in the story of the "Little Descent," and may refer to the settlement of Chichén Itzá by peoples from the east coast. Here the Venus sign is not just a vague astronomical reference but a reference to a group of people (Miller, 1976).

The platform was most likely used for ritual dances, but it also may have been used for drama. Landa describes "two small stages of hewn stone" at Chichén, "with four staircases, paved on top, where they say farces were represented, and comedies for the pleasure of the public." These were probably the Platform of the Tigers and Eagles and the Venus platform.

Platform of the Tigers and Eagles

Platform of the Tigers and Eagles

Between the Castillo and the Ball Court is a small square platform with stairs on four sides called Platform of the Tigers and Eagles. It is similar to the Venus Platform, but smaller, and was constructed about A.D. 1200.

On the *alfardas* of the stairway are representations of the feathered serpent, Quetzalcoatl, known to the Mayas as Kukulcán. At the top of the stairway, serpents' heads protrude from the cornice molding. The structure exemplifies the Mexican Order of Tigers (Jaguars) and Eagles.

The Jaguar-Eagle cult was unknown to the Classic Mayas. The order was introduced by the Mexicans, and its concept dominated Post-Classic Chichén Itzá. "Of the greatest importance in the religion of these people was the Jaguar-Eagle cult," said Alfred M. Tozzer. ". . . The members wore the skin of the jaguar and the feathers of the eagle, and carried the insignia of their order on their shields and banners. The warriors were associated with the sun god, Tonatiuh, and were considered his servants. For mankind to live, the sun must cross the heavens daily and so must have sustenance consisting of human blood and hearts (1957: 129)."

The architecture and art we see in modified florescent Chichén Itzá was influenced by this concept of sustaining the sun by sacrifice and the domination of the culture by a warrior caste.

Tzompantli (Chichén Itzá)

Tzompantli Eagle

Tzompantli

In the Nahuatl language of the Aztecs, *tzompantli* means "wall of skulls." The skulls of the sacrificial victims were displayed in racks on this platform. Note that although these are representations of skulls, they are all depicted with eyes, and although they are anatomically incorrect, the effect is by no means diminished. The lower molding, frieze, and upper molding are decorated with skulls.

Other portions of the wall display eagles and feathered serpents. Here we see an eagle eating, apparently with relish, a human heart. The sacrificial offering of the human heart is likely made to Tlalchitonatiuh, the Mexican god of the rising sun. In the context of this platform, the sacrifice probably took place in connection with a ritual dance in which the participants were dressed as tigers and eagles and the victim was a prisoner of war. The basic concept involved was to replenish the power of the sun with human blood.

The victims were not unwilling in all cases. The captured warrior who was filled with religious fervor welcomed death in order to perpetuate the sun and, therefore, the world, much as early Christian martyrs, who died at the hands of the Romans, or Islamic warriors, who died fighting the infidel, welcomed death.

Here pictured is a Mayanized-Mexican warrior with a speech scroll coming from his mouth. He is depicted wearing a characteristic costume with a headdress and a disk ornament on his back. Serpents project in front of him.

Like the Venus Platform and the Platform of the Tigers and Eagles, the Tzompantli was probably used for ceremonial music and dance in addition to the display of skulls. This Tzompantli demonstrates the Mexican Indian's preoccupation with death. Since we all are, to a greater or lesser degree, fascinated by or concerned with death, this structure has a grim attraction for everyone who views it.

These three structures were probably constructed between A.D. 1050 and 1200.

Tzompantli Warrior

151

Temple of the Warriors (Chichén Itzá)

Temple of the Warriors

From the Castillo may be seen the Temple of the Warriors, facing west toward the great plaza. It is a splendid building resting upon a stepped platform surrounded by colonnaded halls. "It is closely planned after Pyramid 'B' at Tula (Coe, 1966: 124)." Clearly the greater size and superior workmanship of the Chichén Itzá Warriors' Temple demonstrate that the Mexican intruders made good use of Maya architectural and sculptural tradition.

This construction came to the Mayas as a result of the Mexican influence. Tatiana Proskouriakoff explains it thus: "By using the column as a structural support, they could span a room with several parallel vaults, permitting free circulation inside and providing ample lighting from the colonnaded façade. The use of the wooden lintel, with which they were already familiar, allowed a span large enough to make construction spacious as well as practicable (1963: 99)."

This building marked a fundamental change in the Maya philosophy of building. Up to this point Maya architecture had always been outward looking. Here we have a building designed to be utilized on the inside. At Chichén the Mexican warriors achieved equal status with the priests and built halls big

Temple of the Warriors (aerial view)

enough to be used by large numbers of people.

While the Temple of the Warriors was being restored in 1926, another structure was discovered underneath, in the same position as the subtemple under the Castillo. It is called the Chacmool Temple. The colors of the columns of the inner structure have been preserved. While the upper temple was being excavated, several mural paintings, two of which show a village on the sea and an attack, were found and removed. These paintings may refer to the legend of the "Little Descent" people from the east (Miller, 1976).

The pyramid on which the temple stands is in three tiers with a single stairway on the west facing the great plaza. On the west and south are the round and square columns which make up the colonnades known as the Group of the Thousand Columns. The portion of the Temple of the Thousand Columns facing the plaza is called the North Colonnade. It is 600 feet by 75 feet. This colonnade was one of the first columned structures of this type constructed by the Mayas. "It was a radical innovation, and we may judge from the Group of the Thousand Columns that it gained great popularity at Chichén Itzá (Proskouriakoff, 1963: 100)."

Temple of the Warriors (south view)

This view of the Temple of the Warriors shows the parallel line of the Mayanized-Mexican architecture. There are no rounded corners here. Beginning with the base of the Thousand Columns Hall, which is in two courses, through the pyramid and the Temple of Warriors on its summit, the line is straight, hard, and parallel. The only Classic Maya concept left in this view is the corbel-vaulted passageway under the hall from north to south at the east end of the colonnade, which measures 320 by 75 feet.

On the west side of the building immediately in front of the stairway that leads to the temple entrance is a series of columns depicting warriors in low relief. Note the military arrogance of the head and facial expression of the warrior shown. Here stands a warrior in full regalia with a huge quetzal-feather headdress. His eyes, nose, and mouth tell us he is a conqueror. Below him is what appears to be the Mexican representation of the fork-tongued feathered serpent.

The warrior is facing west as if he were

Man-Bird-Serpent

Mexican Warrior

coming from the east. This is true of most of the figures depicted in connection with this temple. Where it was possible, figures were drawn facing west, further evidence that they

refer to the "Little Descent" legend of the founders of Chichén Itzá coming from the east coast of the Yucatán peninsula (Miller, 1976c).

The eyes of this warrior are almond shaped, with the epicanthic eyefold of the Mesoamerican Indians who came from northeastern Asia across the Alaska land bridge to the Western Hemisphere as early as forty thousand years ago.

The crouching man-bird-serpent is represented at Chichén some three hundred times, and it appears on the upper level of the temple. This symbol represents Venus as the morning star and is also identified with the group which came to Chichén Itzá from the east coast. These people were one of the groups which made up the allies who dominated Chichén Itzá and the surrounding area during the Modified Florescent period (Miller, 1976b).

155

Chacmool and View of Castillo

The platform at the top of the Pyramid of the Warriors supports the Temple of the Warriors, in front of which sits the most definitive Mexican symbol, the chacmool. The name can be translated "red tiger" and was conferred by Augustus Le Plongeon when he discovered one during the excavation of the Platform of the Eagles.

Another symbol of the Mexican invasion is the standard bearer, here pictured just above the serpent's head at the top of the stair *alfarda*. This figure was used to hold a ceremonial banner.

Standard Bearer (Temple of the Warriors)

Temple of the Warriors (Temple Entrance)

The decoration of the west façade of the Temple of the Warriors combines Classic Maya with Mexican motifs and demonstrates the amalgamation of the cultures. The face of the building displays masks in the traditional Maya style—stylized eyes, ears, and teeth, together with a curved proboscis. The basic style is Puuc, with a plain lower façade and a decorated frieze above. In addition, however, are the two feathered-serpent columns with heads like dragons facing the chacmool, who reclines looking westward to the plaza. This grouping of combined Classic Maya and Maya-Mexican symbols of religious fervor constituted a backdrop for the ceremonies which doubtlessly included the deposition, on the receptical formed by the chacmool's stomach, of excised and bleeding hearts. Traces of the red color of the serpent's mouth are still visible. At the time of these ceremonies, nearly one thousand years ago, it was flaming red— terrible and menacing.

In the older Temple of the Chacmool beneath this one the original colors of sculptured pillars are still visible, but the wall paintings showing an audience scene with Mayanized-Mexicans seated on thrones have disappeared. This temple is coeval with the unexcavated Temple of the Tables to the north. It is two-chambered, each room divided into two columnar ranges which support double corbel vaults.

Chacmool
(Temple of the
Warriors)

159

Atlantean Table (Temple of the Warriors)

In the rear of the inner room on the east side of the Temple of the Warriors is a rectangular stone altar or table supported by atlanteans. They are small columns, at the top of which head and arms are sculptured to support the altar. Each figure is slightly different from the others. The fit is not exact, and some have shims of small stones to level the table. Some were longer than others. Note the sullen features and Oriental eyes of the atlantean in the detail photograph reproduced here.

The temple sanctuary and antechamber contain pillars carved with representations of the earth monster and warriors, which supported a Maya-type vaulted ceiling. The door jambs are carved to represent a god with a human mask and serpent's tongue.

The Temple of the Warriors was constructed on a pyramid which, at its base, was approximately 130 feet square; it is of stepped design with four recessed terraces. On the south side of the pyramid, which has been stabilized and restored, are a series of panels with low-relief

160

Tigers and Eagles

representations of jaguars and eagles devouring human hearts. The photograph shows an eagle to the left, a jaguar in the center, and an eagle to the right; each has a representation of a human heart in paw or claw with mouth or beak open.

This series of panels is done with great skill and furnishes an insight into the Mayanized-Mexican culture of the Yucatán, but glyphs were not used. Classic period Maya glyph writing was not utilized in stone by the Mayanized-Mexicans although glyphs were used in codices. This departure from the Classic Maya technique of inscribing glyphs in stone makes it more difficult for the archaeologist to correlate the sequence of history and building during the Post-Classic period at Chichén Itzá.

Between the masks which appear at intervals on the temple façade are representations of the serpent with his great forked tongue and a human head in his widespread jaws.

Temple of the Warriors (south wall detail)

161

Well of Sacrifice

Well of Sacrifice

Five hundred and fifty yards north of the Castillo at the end of the *sacbe* is a *cenote* which is the famous, or perhaps infamous, "Well of Sacrifice" of Chichén Itzá. The ancient Mayas artificially rounded the *cenote* to produce a circular hole in the limestone approximately 285 feet in diameter and 60 feet from rim to water level. The maximum depth of the water is approximately 40 feet. On the south side of the well is a small temple called the Temple of Xtoloc (the lizard).

The Well of Sacrifice is mentioned by Bishop Landa, who wrote: "Into this well, they have had, and then had, the custom of throwing men alive as a sacrifice to the gods, in times of drought, and they believed that they did not die though they never saw them again. They also threw into it . . . other things, like precious stones and things which they prized."

The Franciscan Tomas López Medel (1612) wrote that in times when rain was needed for their maize, the natives made sacrifice "with the death and offering of one or two Indian virgins . . . and they placed her in a shrine which was near there, where the priest withdrew her . . . and they brought her forth from there, and having tied her with a long rope, they lowered her down to the depth of the water, ducking her many times until they drowned her."

Of the skeletal material recovered from the cenote, thirteen were males, eight were females; one was middle-aged, six were young adults, and one was a sub-adult (eighteen to twenty years of age). There were fourteen skulls of children.

Other objects recovered from the *cenote* included embossed gold disks, copper bells, some gold and silver, jade jewelry, rock crystal, amber utensils, carved bone, and mother-of-pearl. There is no way to estimate when these objects were offered since the well was a place of pilgrimage and sacrifice from the seventh to the sixteenth century, and possibly later. One carved jade piece recovered was carved at Piedras Negras, dated A.D. 706, and another recovered item was a Palenque jade bead dated A.D. 690.

El Mercado (Chichén Itzá)

El Mercado

El Mercado, the market, lies about 450 feet to the south of the Temple of the Warriors. It was so named because it reminded the Spaniards of the open markets of Spain, and it was probably actually a market. At the time of excavation, "when some of the debris was cleared away, the floor of the court showed numerous traces of small constructions that may well have served as temporary booths (Proskouriakoff, 1963: 103)." The colonnade may also have served as a place for holding court.

The building was constructed in the later Mexican period and made up the south boundary of the great plaza of the Thousand Columns. This area of Chichén, lying to the southeast of the Castillo and the great central plaza, is all Maya-Mexican.

El Mercado

The Mercado consists of a long colonnade constructed on a 250-foot-long raised platform oriented east and west. There are stairs on the north, east, and west. Round columns and square pillars alternate along the course of the platform. To the rear (south) of this long portico is a square building with a peristyle of tall, delicate, round columns surrounding a central court and impluvium. Probably the court was roofed with palms, as no stones which could have belonged to a roof have been found.

Steam Bath

Steam Bath

The Steam Bath, or Sweat House, is located to the east of the plaza of the Thousand Columns and the Mercado. The south portion of the building is a small portico with benches which served as the waiting room for the bathers. A small steam room to the north contained two benches and a place for the hot rocks which produced the steam when sprinkled with water. The oven for heating the stones is in the rear. There is a canal under the floor to carry off the excess water and two small windows for ventilation.

The building is of Puuc design, without decoration except for a tripartite medial and cornice molding. The cornice molding also has a negative batter in the upper course. This small building, built for secular rather than religious purposes, is a jewel of simplicity.

Southeast Colonnade

Southeast Colonnade

To the east of the Mercado is a group of columns called the Southeast Colonnade. It has an interesting atrium surrounded by a limestone-block wall with a series of engaged round columns and square capitals. The columns make up a part of the wall of the atrium.

There are several benches, a painted capstone, and some atlantean figures in the building. The secondary walls which run from pillar to pillar make up seven rooms and the southern part of the colonnade.

High Priest's Grave

High Priest's Grave

This pyramid is south of the highway, but it is part of the Maya-Mexican complex. Both pyramid and temple were constructed in the Mexican period before A.D. 1050. It is also often referred to as the *Osario*, which is the Spanish word for ossuary, a depository for the bones of the dead. Its style is transitional between the Castillo and Temple of the Warriors. Originally the pyramid had four radiating staircases built in the same way as those on the Castillo, but the structure has not been restored. On the top was a temple with a center sanctuary surrounded by a gallery with a portico facing east.

A climb to the top reveals a shaft leading down through the center of the pyramid pile. The shaft is stone lined and vertical and extends down to the base of the pyramid. There is a small opening with some stone steps that lead into a cave about thirty-six feet deep.

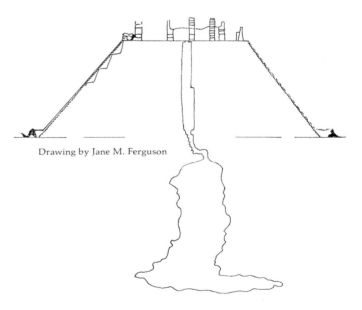

Drawing by Jane M. Ferguson

During excavation, seven tombs were found containing skeletons and funerary offerings which included jade, rock crystal, and copper bells.

The remaining pillars on the pyramid platform are decorated with the feathered serpent and Maya-Mexican figures.

167

Caracol (Chichén Itzá)

Caracol

On the south side of the highway that bisects the ruins of Chichén Itzá is the Classic Maya area. The unique building in this portion of Chichén Itzá is the Caracol, which means "snail" or "winding staircase."

Construction of the substructure of the Caracol was completed in the late Maya Classic stage between A.D. 600 and 850. The base platform is Puuc Style and is Maya, but the building over all is the oldest Maya-Mexican structure at Chichén. The facings are an integral part of the masonry, and the structure has

168

an overhanging apron-type cornice molding. This, too, is Maya. Sylvanus G. Morley found a stela between two divisions of the upper stairway in 1923 which he dated about A.D. 840. We can assume from this that by A.D. 840 much of the building was completed.

The unique element of this building is the round observatory with its equally unique five-member medial molding and spiral staircase. This portion of the Caracol is Maya-Mexican and indicates the building was used and remodeled for at least four hundred years from A.D. 800 to 1200.

A circular tower forty-eight feet high was added to the substructure platform. Part of the substructure is the great stairway on the west side (here facing the observer). The lower course of the tower was solid. The second circular course contains two galleries with a spiral staircase leading to the observatory. The stairway starts at the height of the vaulting and continues upward to the observatory. In order to protect this magnificent structure, it has been necessary to close the spiral stairway. These very ancient buildings suffer from the traffic of tourists and require protection and repair; visitors should understand that some restraints are necessary to preserve these ruins of the Mayas for posterity.

Stylized masks are located above the four doorways to the tower. Above the proboscis and between the eyes of each is an anthropomorphic face. Across the top of the mask is a fillet, or upper molding, composed of eight rings through which is woven a plain band with points on each end. This mask is basically Puuc-Maya.

The tower constituted an observatory. The plan of the windows and shafts leading to the windows are oriented to indicate the azimuths for south, west, the equinoxes, and the summer solstice.

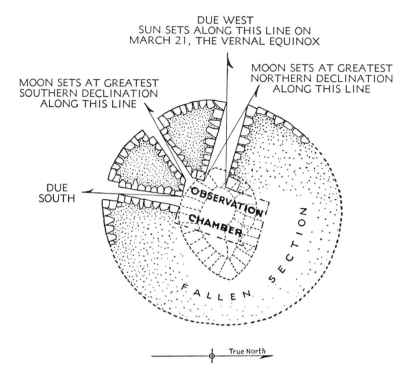

From Morley and Brainerd, *The Ancient Maya*

The Observatory of the Caracol

Caracol and Nunnery Complex (Chichén Itzá)

George Kubler suggests that there is no counterpart at Tula of the early Mexican (Toltec) architecture of Chichén Itzá, of which the Caracol is an excellent example, and that, therefore, Tula, in central Mexico, may have been merely an outpost of the Yucatán Toltec civilization. What he is saying is that the generally accepted theory that the Toltecs came from Tula and overran Chichén may be in error, that in fact the Toltec civilization developed at Chichén and was extended to central Mexico (1975: 188). Alfred Tozzer recognizes the problem of the origin of the Toltecs, but says, "Wherever may have been the point of original dispersal of the Toltec, the best evidence is that the origin of the material culture known as Toltec was at Tula on the Mexican plateau (1957: 27)." J. Eric S. Thompson believes that the Itzás were the Chontal Mayas who had been subject to Mexican influence. But whatever the direction of the influence, whether from the east or from the west, "evidence from George F. Andrews' work at Dzibilchaltún suggests that the arrival of Mexican influence in Yucatán is at least two centuries earlier than the founding of Chichén Itzá (Miller, 1976: personal communication)."

Nunnery

The Nunnery Complex (Monjas)

The Nunnery complex is probably the oldest and in many ways the most significant of all the structures at Chichén Itzá. Consider first the huge rectangular building behind the stairway and beneath the superimposed temple. Within this massive structure are at least two earlier platforms, each probably one-storied, the oldest of which is probably contemporary with the founding of Chichén. This would place construction as early as A.D. 600 or, if we follow Morley, even earlier. He says, "Chichén Itzá [was] occupied by the Itzá" on "9.4.0.0.0, 13 Ahau 18 Yax," the Gregorian equivalent of which is October 18, A.D. 514.

The structure was named by the Spaniards because the multi-chambered building reminded them of the convents in Spain.

The initial building was constructed on a platform thirty feet high. It had two wings which were divided into chambers with two additional chambers at each end. Next the substructure was widened and a second floor was added, covering the roof comb of the original building, and a stairway sculptured with animals was constructed. The rooms were filled with rubble to give additional

Nunnery Annex

support to the structures above. The decoration of these buildings consisted of indented stepped frets and floral designs.

Constructed contemporaneously with the principal building was a building to the east in typically Classic Maya of Chenes style. It is referred to as the Nunnery Annex. The lower façade below the medial molding is decorated with lattice work, and the upper façade has a series of masks. The portal of the east entrance is just below the monster mask. The mask is also repeated on the lower façade and the building corners up to the molding, and is repeated again up to the cornice molding. Over the door is either a human or an anthropomorphic figure wearing a huge feathered headdress.

Looking again to the main structure, one sees that it now appears as modified by the Maya-Mexicans—the Maya period ended in the ninth century. The last Long Count date (10.3.0.0.0—A.D. 899) is connected with the Nunnery. The grand stairway on the north side of the Nunnery and the temple on the upper platforms are Mexican. The third story was built of reused stones and dates from the last of the twelfth century.

One of the most interesting features of this structure is the great gash in the building on the right side of the grand stairway where Augustus Le Plongeon (1826–1908)—who discovered and named the original chacmool—dynamited his way into the core of the Monjas revealing the inner structure.

172

Nunnery Annex Detail

The Church (east view)

La Iglesia (the Church)

The Church (Iglesia)

The Iglesia or church, so called because of its proximity to the Nunnery, is primarily Maya, although it may have been rebuilt in part in Post-Classic times. It is a rectangular building containing one room with a single portal on the west.

The lower portion of the building is without decoration. Above the medial molding is a stepped-fret meander which circles the building. Above this is the frieze. On each corner of the building and over the central portal is a stylized Maya mask with curved snout. There are also four figures, one pair on each side of the center mask. They include an armadillo and a snail on the north side and a turtle and a crab on the south. These are the Bacabs, who, according to Maya belief, hold up the sky.

The cornice molding has at its base a molding and a negative-battered upper molding; between the two is a serpent. Above the molding is a roof comb with a frieze made up of masks.

174

Red House

The Red House (Chichanchob)

Chichanchob is the Maya word for "small holes," and this building was possibly so named because of the open lattice work in the roof comb. The Red House is also referred to by the Spanish equivalent, *Casa Colorada*. This name came from the traces of red painted on the wall of the portico.

The temple is constructed on a platform with rounded corners and a central west-facing stairway. The building is Maya. E. Wyllys Andrews reports that radio-carbon tests on "unquestionably original beams from the Iglesia and the Chichanchob . . . have yielded dates of A.D. 600, 610, and 780, ± 70" which indicate that these two buildings were either constructed or repaired during the Middle Classic period.

The outside walls are undecorated, as is the frieze. The only decoration is on the flying façade and the roof comb behind it. The forward roof comb has three masks.

Red House and Caracol (aerial view)

175

House of the Deer

The House of the Deer

This small, unreconstructed building faces the same small plaza as the Red House. The architecture of the two structures is very similar, each constructed on a platform with rounded corners and each with an undecorated façade.

The House of the Deer was given its name because of an interior wall painting depicting a deer, which, unfortunately, is no longer visible. This building was constructed in the Classic Maya period of the seventh and eighth centuries.

Temple of the Wall Panels

Temple of the Wall Panels

Between the Caracol and the Nunnery is the Maya-Mexican building known as the Temple of the Wall Panels because of its sculptured walls. On top of the platform is a portico with two columns behind which was a sanctuary. Originally this temple was reached by stairs from the rear of the ground-level room, which has two rows of columns and benches on three sides. Later the interior steps were removed, and the stairway now to be seen in the front of the building was constructed. It was a typical Mexican stairway with serpent heads and banner holders on the bottom and top of the *alfardas*. This construction is curious because the stairway necessitated passage over the roof of the center room in order to reach the temple.

The plan of this building with its colonnade is similar to that of the Temple of the Warriors.

The wall bas-reliefs were done late in the Mexican period.

177

Akabtzib (west view)

Akabtzib (aerial view)

Akabtzib Glyph Lintel

Akabtzib

Akabtzib means "dark writing" in Maya, and this building was so named because of the reliefs containing a glyphic text which are found on a lintel over an inner doorway on the south side of the building. On the underside is a person seated on a throne. Thompson gives the date as 10.2.0.0.0 (A.D. 869) or 10.3.0.0.0 (889).

The Akabtzib, together with the Nunnery, Red House, and Deer House, are the oldest buildings in this area of Chichén Itzá. The center of this building, with two rooms and three doors, is the oldest part and was the first constructed; the north and south additions were made later at approximately the same time, which we can assume was near the dates ascribed to the lintels—that is, A.D. 869 to 889.

The building is constructed upon a platform which can be seen in the aerial photograph, although it is not as readily recognizable from the ground. It is similar to the Puuc style of Uxmal except for the absence of decoration. The façades are plain. The medial and cornice molding are both three-membered and the upper molding has a negative batter.

The spectacular blue-crowned motmots, with their double stringlike tails and butterfly tips, nest in the chambers of the Akabtzib in the spring and go in and out like spirits of the ancient Maya.

Temple of the Atlantean Columns

The Temple of the Atlantean Columns, or Temple of the Dates, is part of a group of buildings in "old" or "unexcavated" Chichén. This group may be reached by taking the path from the southwest corner of the Nunnery south to the abandoned plantation railroad, and farther on for a total of about 835 yards to a path leaving the railroad to the left (east). Follow this path 175 yards to the date group.

This building is interesting because of the dated lintel. The date inscription is complete with an initial series and has been read as 10.2.9.1.9, 9 Muluc 7 Zac, which corresponds to A.D. 879 (Ruz, 1967: 43). It is the only complete hieroglyphic date inscription in Chichén. Actually these dates do not reveal very much with respect to this building because the atlantean columns upon which the lintel is placed are Maya-Mexican of a much later date. "These Atlanteans are much later than the dated stone which was placed upon them in very modern times," commented Tozzer (1957: 89). Yet the lintel demonstrates that Maya Chichén was a viable entity at the close of the Classic period.

Temple of the Atlantean Columns

Cobá

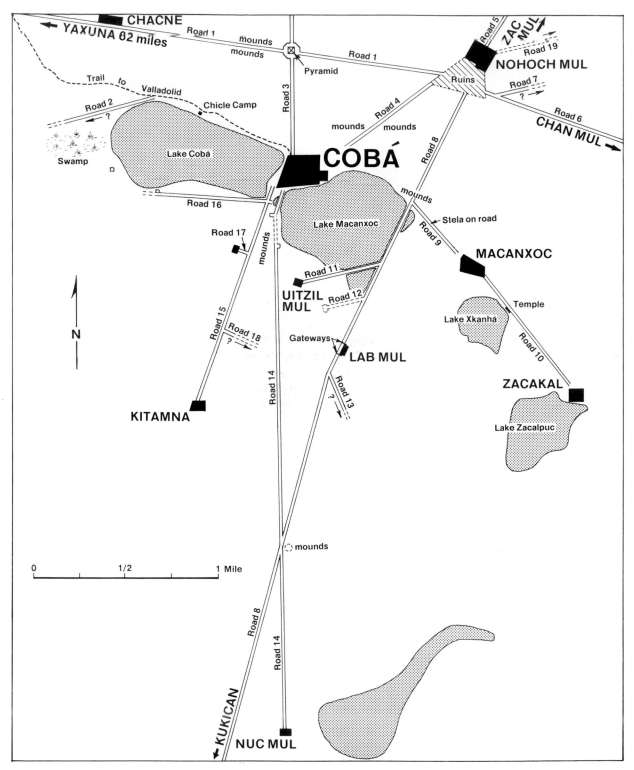

Cobá and Vicinity Road System

Castillo at Cobá, Conjunto Las Pinturas, and Castillo at Nohoch Mul

Three structures, each visible in this picture, have been partly cleared and stabilized at Cobá. In the foreground, next to Lake Macanxoc, is the Castillo of Group B, Cobá. Farther to the southeast along the jeep trail is the small pyramid called the Conjunto Las Pinturas. To the left and east of the Conjunto is the great pyramid and temple of Nohoch Mul.

The Cobá text material was prepared after consultation with and was reviewed by Arthur G. Miller, Research Associate of the Center for Pre-Columbian Studies, Dumbarton Oaks, Washington, D.C. For the past six years, Dr. Miller has directed an intensive archaeological project on the east coast of the Yucatán peninsula with emphasis on Maya mural painting.

Cobá was one of the earliest important Maya Classic period sites in northeastern Yucatán and dates from 9.9.10.0.0 (A.D. 623) according to Morley's dating of Stelae 4 and 6 at Cobá (Morley and Brainerd, 1963: 309). The area is notable for its long period of occupation from as early as A.D. 623 to the late Post-Classic period in the fourteenth or fifteenth century. Many stelae have been located at Cobá: thirty-two Classic period stelae including twenty-three that are sculptured.

In addition, a number of *sacbeob* or raised artificial roads were constructed by the Mayas at Cobá. Sixteen have been discovered which form a network of causeways connecting the central section with outlying centers. The

Conjunto Las Pinturas and Castillo at Nohoch Mul

longest road—over sixty miles—runs westward from Cobá to Yaxuna, southwest of Chichén Itzá. "An important deduction may be made from this causeway. It was built from east to west, from Cobá to Yaxuna, which may indicate that when it was constructed—probably in the early part of the Late Period of the Classic stage—Cobá was the largest city in northeastern Yucatán. This is apparent from the fact that of the seven changes in direction of the highway the first six are made within twenty miles of Cobá in order to pass through smaller settlements dependent on it (Morley and Brainerd, 1963: 310)."

It has been suggested that a *sacbe* ran from Cobá to Xcaret, the point of embarkation for Cozumel, on to the Tancah-Tulum area, but to this date it has not been found.

Cobá was the Maya name for the site and means "water stirred by the wind." The ruins were explored in 1926–29 by Sylvanus G. Morley, J. Eric S. Thompson, Harry E. D. Pollock, and Jean Charlot.

Cobá reached its greatest expansion about 9.10.0.0.0 (A.D. 633). There are "monuments bearing Maya dates from 9.2.0.0.0 (A.D. 475) to 10.2.10.0.0 (A.D. 879) scattered across the northern area at Tulum, Cobá, Chichén Itzá, Dzibilchaltún, Xkalumkin, Oxkintok, and farther south at Xtampak and Etzná (E. W. Andrews, 1965: 305)."

In this view in the foreground is the Post-Classic temple of Conjunto Las Pinturas, constructed after A.D. 800. In the background is the Classic period pyramid of Nohoch Mul built much earlier and topped with a Post-Classic Temple of the Diving God which is similar to the temples at Tulum, built between A.D. 1200 and 1450 (Miller, 1976: personal communication).

Castillo, Cobá

The Castillo

The Castillo at Cobá faces west toward the main plaza and Lake Macanxoc. This pyramid is part of the central group of Cobá, which is just north and east of the isthmus between Lake Cobá and Lake Macanxoc. The area of the ruins which have been designated as Group B at Cobá measures some 1,650 feet east and west and 975 feet north and south.

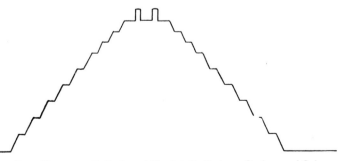

From Thompson, Pollock, and Charlot, *Preliminary Study . . . of Coba*

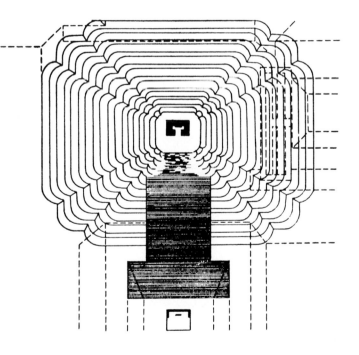

Drawings of Castillo

185

Castillo, Cobá (west view)

The Castillo is a stepped pyramid crowned by a small temple at its summit. This great pyramid is about 129 feet east and west at its base, 166 feet north and south and 78 feet high. The outer walls are constructed of roughly faced stones set in mortar, and the core is probably stone rubble. The surface of the pyramid was originally finished smooth with plaster.

There are nine terraces with inset rounded corners. The stairway continues to the foot of the seventh terrace, beyond which is a wall that rises to the platform which supports the small temple at the top. Where the stairs are absent, there appears to be the wall of an earlier construction. On the platform at the top of the pyramid is a small, single-room building with a door facing west. Inside the structure was found a stela standing against the rear wall. It was badly flaked away and no carving remained.

Stela 11

All of the carved stelae at Cobá are in small shrines. The structure which supports Stela 11 is situated just in front of the Castillo stairway and measures about twelve feet square. At the rear of this small platform was a low wall with extensions at either end projecting about four and one-half feet forward from it.

Stela 11 is approximately four and one-half feet high and three feet wide. The stela is still in place. It was carved on the west face only, but is very much eroded. Originally there were forty-two glyph blocks arranged in six columns of seven glyphs each, but the glyphs are not sufficiently legible to determine the date of erection of the stela.

Stela 11, Castillo, Cobá

187

Conjunto Las Pinturas

Conjunto Las Pinturas

Between the Castillo at Cobá and the No-hoch Mul is a Post-Classic tiered temple with a single stairway rising from a colonnaded area on the north side of the pyramid. On the platform at the summit of the pyramid is a small structure with doors on the east and west and the main portal on the north side which utilizes a single column.

The stone lintel above the column capital and the three horizontal stone courses above the lintel contain the remnants of a mural painting. The building is late Post-Classic.

Painted Lintel

The murals are in codex style; that is to say, they follow the style of existing Maya codices (Miller, 1976: personal communication). Instead of a Maya introductory glyph, the paintings contain a Mexican year sign, evidence that the paintings were made by the Mayanized-Mexicans in the Post-Classic period (Miller, 1976: personal communication). The paintings are not in good condition and are now protected by a thatch covering.

From the east door there is a spectacular view, through a break in the jungle, of Nohoch Mul, which faces squarely the easterly alignment of the Conjunto Las Pinturas.

Castillo at Nohoch Mul (Cobá)

The Castillo at Nohoch Mul

The Nohoch Mul is a group of ruins (Group B) located just over half a mile along a jeep trail to the northeast of the Castillo at Cobá. The Castillo pyramid at Nohoch Mul faces southwest toward Structure X and Stela 20.

The Castillo (Structure I) measures about 180 feet (northeast-southwest) by 198 feet at its base and 78 feet in height. The substructure closely resembles the pyramid of the Castillo at Cobá. The pyramid is of the Classic period of Maya culture and is similar in design and style to the pyramids at Tikal in the Petén area of Guatemala.

The great stairway is about thirty-six feet

wide and rises on the southern side of the pyramid past six terraces to the foot of the final terrace, where two small flights of stairs branch in opposite directions and lead to the platform on top. The temple is Maya East Coast type and is similar in style to the structures at Tulum, which would indicate construction some time after A.D. 1200. This "suggests that the temple, the small stairway, and possibly the entire platform at the top of the pyramid form a late addition to the original structure (Thompson, Pollock, and Charlot, 1932: 82)."

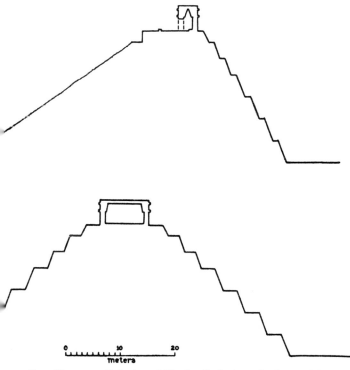

From Thompson, Pollock, and Charlot, *Preliminary Study . . . of Coba*

Cross-section of Castillo, Nohoch Mul

Castillo at Nohoch Mul from Structure X

191

Temple, Castillo at Nohoch Mul

Temple, Structure I, Nohoch Mul

The temple on the platform at the top of the Castillo at Nohoch Mul is of the late Post-Classic style of the east coast of Yucatán. Since it is similar to the style of Tulum, it is probable that construction took place after A.D. 1200. In addition, the façade of the temple has two extant sunken panels containing figures of the Diving God in the form and style of Tulum.

The temple is situated at the back of the platform which is approximately forty-five feet wide by thirty-six feet deep. In front of the temple is a small built-up altar. Originally, the temple had three sunken panels, only two of which remain. There is a single doorway and inside is a single corbel-vaulted room.

Temple, Castillo at Nohoch Mul

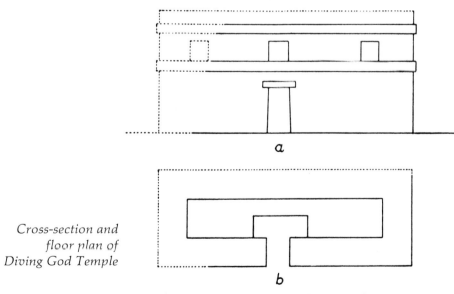

Cross-section and floor plan of Diving God Temple

From Thompson, Pollock, and Charlot, *Preliminary Study . . . of Coba*

193

Structure X (Cobá)

Structure X

This structure is near the foot of the great pyramid of Nohoch Mul. In front of it is the magnificent Stela 20.

Stela 20, Structure X

Stela 20, Bound Figure

Stela 20 bears the date 9.12.12.0.5 (A.D. 684). The stela, which was found in 1930, had fallen face down, but had originally faced west and has been reset in that position. Only the front is carved, and by virtue of the fact that the stela fell face down, it is well preserved. The carving shows a central figure with main panels of glyphs down the sides and other glyphs inset from the bases of the two vertical panels. The body of the main figure faces the front with its head in profile. The figure wears a lower garment of jaguar skin, necklaces, arm-bands, and sandals. There is a ceremonial bar held across the chest.

Two small kneeling figures face in toward the main figure with bound hands raised in supplication. The feet of the main figure rest on the backs of two small figures which are on all fours and back to back. There is a band of glyphs between the feet of the main figure and the backs of the supporters.

This stela represents the style of Cobá, which is epitomized by the more or less rigid conventions of the diagonal position of the serpent bar and the stiff pose of the main figure, with small bound prisoners at his feet.

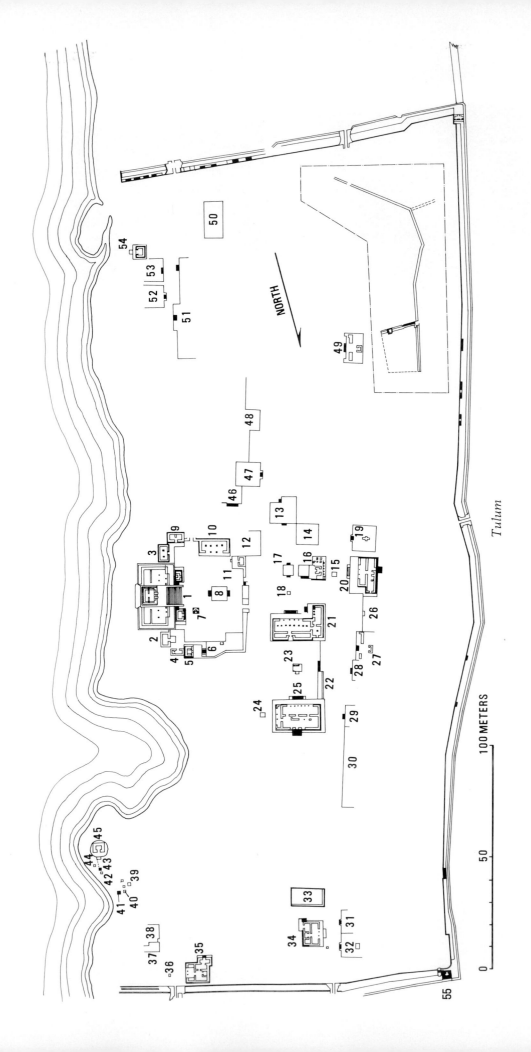

Tulum

NORTH

100 METERS

Tulum

Tulum from the Southeast

This aerial view of Tulum is from the southeast over the Caribbean Sea. The center structure is the Castillo, and across the top of the photograph is a portion of the wall which surrounds the old city.

The text on Tulum was prepared after consultation with and was reviewed by Arthur G. Miller, Research Associate of the Center for Pre-Columbian Studies, Dumbarton Oaks, Washington, D.C. Dr. Miller has been engaged in archaeological research at Tulum from 1971 through 1975, primarily sponsored by Dumbarton Oaks and the National Geographic Society.

On May 7, 1518, an expedition led by Juan de Grijalva sailed along the coast of Yucatán, where Juan Díaz reported his ships passed "three large towns separated from each other by about two miles. There were many houses of stone, very tall towers, and buildings covered with straw." The report continued, "We followed the shore day and night, and the next day towards sunset we perceived a city or town so large that Seville would not have seemed more considerable nor better." It is thought that the city so described was Tulum.

The ruins are situated on the east coast of

Tulum from the West

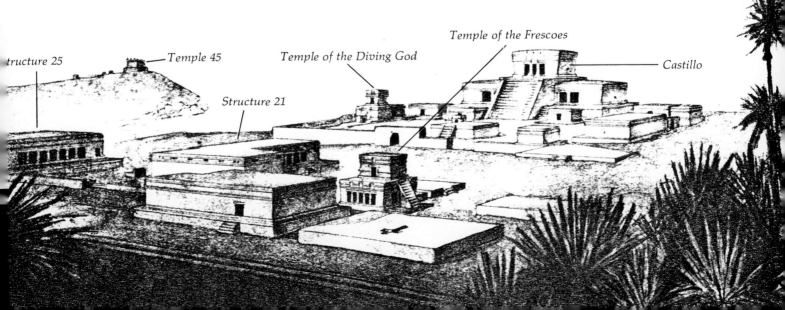

tructure 25   Temple 45   Structure 21   Temple of the Diving God   Temple of the Frescoes   Castillo

Quintana Roo about forty miles south of Playa del Carmen. There is an excellent hard-surface road between Cancún and Tulum.

The ruins stand on the summit of a limestone cliff some 40 feet high. The land slopes away from the cliff and then rises again to form a ridge about 600 feet from the cliff. The central portion, which we see here, is enclosed by a great wall, a part of which can be seen in the background. The wall follows the ridge for about 1,266 feet and is connected with the cliff by perpendicular walls approximately 550 feet long which form a rectangle enclosing the buildings. The layout of the city was dictated by these rectangular walls.

The Castillo is visible for many miles at sea and is shown on navigation charts of the Yucatán coast. To the right of the Castillo is a small cove with a beautiful beach for swimming.

Tulum means "wall" or "rampart," a name given to the site in modern times because of the wall which surrounds it. The Maya name was Zamá, meaning "dawn"—an appropriate name for a city facing east to the sea.

In this view the two-story structure with four columns in the foreground is the Temple of the Frescoes; in the center, in the background, overlooking the Caribbean is the Castillo, and the smaller two-story building to the left of the Castillo is the Temple of the Diving God.

Tulum is a relatively small site and is of the Maya Post-Classic period. It is now established that the site was first occupied about A.D. 1200 and that the stela found in front of the Temple of the Initial Series bearing the date 9.6.10.0.0 (A.D. 564), was brought in from another site, probably Tancah. (E. W. Andrews, 1965: 299 and Miller, 1976: personal communication).

Recent archaeological research carried out in the Tulum area from 1971 through 1975 directed by Arthur G. Miller has provided mural painting, architectural, and ceramic evidence confirming the date of establishment of Tulum. The Temple of the Frescoes and the Temple of the Diving God were erected as late as A.D. 1450. After the Spanish Conquest the area was used as a ceremonial center by the fiercely independent local Mayas well into the twentieth century (Miller, 1976: personal communication).

Tulum is a walled city and likely was an incipient urban center more than simply a ceremonial center, as there are indications of dwellings inside the walls and evidence that Structures 21 and 25 were adaptable as residences. In addition, the layout of the site indicates that there may have been an avenue or street from the northwest portal in the wall to a counterpart in the south wall.

Tulum was constructed by the Mayanized-Mexicans who were occupying the east coast of Yucatán (Quintana Roo) at the end of the Classic period and the beginning of the Post-Classic period. Cobá, Xelha, and Tancah were Classic period Maya sites in the area. For three or four hundred years before Tulum the east coast had been subjected to incursions from outside the area, and the social organization and architecture of the Modified Florescent or Post-Classic period of Maya culture was the result of the coalescence of factions following long periods of internecine warfare among the commercial elements of the Mexican and Maya civilizations of the east coast (Miller, 1976: personal communication).

The heart of the ceremonial center of Tulum is circumscribed on the west by a low ceremonial wall which can be seen in this aerial view. Within this precinct are Structures 1 (the Castillo) through 11, and includes the Temple of the Diving God on the north side and the Temple of the Initial Series on the south.

North Wall and Northeast Gate

The Wall

Tulum was protected by a rampart which guarded the landward sides of the city on the north, west, and south. The east side was naturally fortified by approximately 40 feet of sharp and jutting rocks which rise from the Caribbean. The area inside the ramparts is about 1,260 feet north to south and 540 feet east to west. There were five entrances, two of which are pictured here, each covered with slabs.

The walls vary from ten feet to seventeen feet high and average about twenty feet in thickness. On the top of the wall was a walkway protected by a parapet which was reached by stairways placed at intervals around the inner side.

Small temples were constructed at the northwest and southwest corners of the wall. Beginning at the southwest corner, another wall extended south and east to about 105 feet from the shore.

Wall and West Gate

201

Temple of the Frescoes (West view)

Temple of the Frescoes

The Temple of the Frescoes (Structure 16) is the most interesting structure at Tulum because of the preserved mural paintings on the west wall inside the gallery. This temple was constructed in the Late Post-Classic period, probably about 1450 (Miller, 1976: personal communication).

On the ground floor is a single room with an entrance on the west and a small altar at the back. This room is surrounded by a gallery on the north, east, and south sides with a four-column entrance on the west and two pillars on the south. A temple was constructed on the top with its entrance to the west, and may have been reached by a stairway on the south which is now destroyed. Mural paintings decorate the façade of the inner temple.

The outer façade of the temple, above the lintel over the column capitals, was decorated with polychrome figures in stucco. There are three recessed niches over the entrance which contained the Diving God in the center and seated figures with elaborate headdresses on the sides. Red hand prints are visible on the façade above. Between the moldings and the niches are two stucco low reliefs which appear to represent figures enveloped in an interlaced design.

Central Niche Diving God, Temple of the Frescoes

North Niche Figure, Temple of the Frescoes

Detail, Temple of the Frescoes West Façade (Diving God)

The northwest and southwest corners of the cornice are sculptured into gigantic masks in low relief. The mouth and chin are a part of the lower horizontal line, the nose and eye fill the intermolding space, and the headdress is located on the upper course. The face was once painted orange, red, and black and has been tentatively identified as Kukulcán, the feathered serpent; it has also been suggested that it may be Itzamná, the sky god.

The upper story is a single-room structure with an opening to the west. The walls show a definite outward batter and the niche may have contained a stucco figure of the Diving God.

Mask, Temple of the Frescoes

Temple of the Frescoes (Mural Paintings)

On the inner wall of the Temple of the Frescoes behind the four columns are codex-type wall paintings, which, generally speaking, portray Maya gods, goddesses, upper, middle, and lower world representations, a marine scene, and the iconography of birth and rebirth. These paintings were done late in the Post-Classic period, probably after A.D. 1450 (Miller, 1976: personal communication).

Beginning at the extreme left at the north end of the top panel, just beneath the molding, is a representation of *colorín* beans (Miller, 1976: personal communication). Just inside the panel is God D, Itzamná, head of the Maya pantheon, with a serpent in his hand. Facing him in the center of the top panel is another representation of Itzamná with a headdress representing corn. These are kan signs which refer to corn or are the glyph for corn. To the right of this god is the god Chaac, the rain god, who is also referred to as God B. Chaac's headdress is formed of God K's head, crowned with the corn symbol, and there is a ceremonial bar across his chest. Beneath Chaac is a tun (360-day) glyph. At the base of this and each of the panels, except the base panel depicting marine life, are representations of interlaced cords which may, as representations of umbilical cords, refer to birth and rebirth (Miller, 1976: personal communication).

Mural Paintings, upper panel, Itzamná and Chaac

Upper panel

From Lothrop, *Tulum*

Itzamná (God)   Itzamná   Chaac (God B)   Colorin Beans

Mural Paintings, center panel (left), figure with corn-sign feet

The center panel is divided into two panels by twisted cords which have been called serpents. At the extreme left is a small figure whose feet are the corn signs. On his right is a figure whose identity has not been established. The figure is seated on a four-legged creature which appears to be moving. In his headdress are corn signs. Next to this figure is a container which displays three kan signs.

To the right of the twisted cords is the Goddess Ixchel, with a figure of Chaac in each hand and *colorín* bean pods behind her.

In the lower panel only one figure is still discernible and is most likely the seated goddess Ixchel, wife of Itzamná and goddess of childbirth and weaving, and perhaps the moon goddess as well.

Center panel (right), Goddess Ixchel

Center panel

Figure with   *Unknown god on*   *Ixchel*
corn-sign feet   *four-legged animal*

Mural Paintings, lower panel (right), Goddess Ixchel

Lower panel

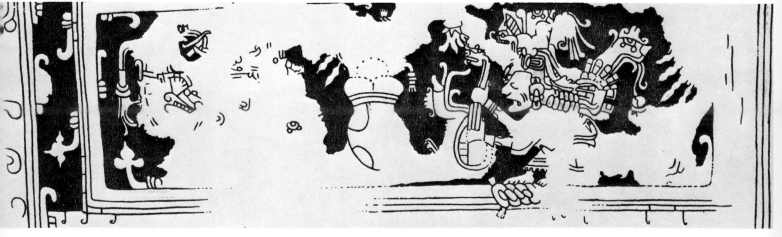

Ixchel

Mural Paintings, lower border (right), manta ray

At the base of the mural is a marine scene which depicts several sea creatures. To the left is a representation of a fish and shown here is a stylized ray.

Maya Deities from the Codices, from left to right: Itzamná, Ixchel, Chaac, God K

The four deities depicted here appear in the mural of the Temple of the Frescoes.

Ixchel, goddess of the moon, medicine, and childbirth, is particularly associated with the east coast of Yucatán. On nearby Cozumel there was a shrine sacred to her which was the object of religious pilgrimages by the Mayas. As she represents birth and rebirth in the iconography of Tulum she may also signify a concept of the rebirth of the Maya civilization of the Post-Classic era.

Itzamná and Ixchel were purely Maya deities. Itzamná was a sky god and was a deity of rain and crops. Chaac is also a sky god of rain whose chief attribute is his long nose.

God K has Mexican connections; he is associated with Chaac and with Texcatlipoca. He is shown here holding a decapitated turkey and is referred to as the "flare god" because he is usually depicted with a flare protruding from his forehead. (See also pages 9 and 10.)

Stela 2 (Temple of the Frescoes)

The ruins of an altar or small platform mound stands in front (on the west side) of the Temple of the Frescoes and supports a stela which has been designated by S. K. Lothrop as Stela 2. It is 4.25 feet high and bears the Short Count date of Katun 2 Ahau.

It is difficult to correlate Maya Short Count dates because they present a similar problem to that which "'76," would present to a historian a thousand years from now—would it, for example, refer to 1776, 1876, or 1976? Commenting on the Stela 2 date, Lothrop said, "Our correlation with Christian chronology, then, must be based on the following: Katun 2 Ahau ended in A.D. 1004, 1261, and 1517. The early date here may be ruled out of consideration because there is neither historic nor stylistic evidence to connect it with this stela at present." He determined that 1517 was too late and concluded, "Granted, then, that 1004 and 1517 are both unlikely, the correct reading is probably A.D. 1261. The style of the monument, which resembles the Mayapán stelae, makes this date quite satisfactory (Lothrop, 1924: 44)."

Stela 2

Structure 20

Structure 20

Structure 20 is just to the west of the Temple of the Frescoes across the main street of the complex and faces east. The substructure is four feet high. On the east side of the building is a flight of steps flanked by wide *alfardas*. The building is the palace type and is comprised of three rooms and a small sanctuary.

The Inner Courtyard Wall

The inner courtyard, dominated by the Castillo on the east, is surrounded by a low wall, the south entrance of which is pictured here. It is probable that this wall delineated a ceremonial center in the heart of the city; it was not designed for defense because it is not very high and there appear to have been gaps between several of the buildings which would have allowed access to the enclosed area.

Northwest View of Inner Courtyard

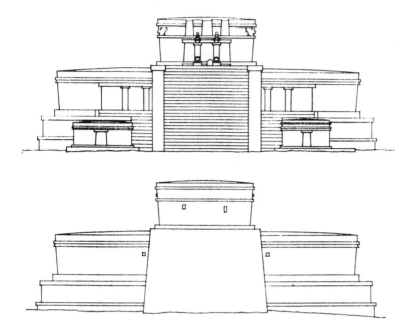

The Castillo

The Castillo (Structure 1) was named by Stephens when he visited the site in the 1840's and was probably the "very large tower" seen by Grijalva and described by Juan Díaz in 1517.

The oldest part of the Castillo now forms the wings which extend north and south from the main stairway. These wings were originally the ends of a large palace similar to Structures 21 and 25 which lie north of the Temple of the Frescoes. The original palace stood on a platform about ten feet high and consisted of two long, narrow rooms with columns in the entrance and a row of columns in the long axis of the outer room. The upper portion of the Castillo was subsequently erected over the palace-type structure, and thereafter two small structures were built at ground level on either side of the stairway.

The main stairway is thirty feet wide and twenty-five feet high and leads to the terrace upon which is located a two-room temple. In front of the temple is a "small upright stone which apparently served as a sacrificial stone on which the victims were extended while the priests tore out their hearts in the sight of the populace in the inner enclosure below (Lothrop, 1924: 77)."

Drawings of east and west elevations (above) of the Castillo and cross-sections (below)

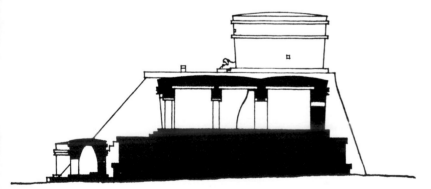

From Lothrop, *Tulum*

The Castillo (west view)

Temple (Castillo upper level)

The entrance to the temple is divided by two serpent columns. Above the three doors are sunken niches. The central figure is the Diving God, the north figure is standing erect, and the south figure has disappeared.

218

Castillo Niche Figure

Temple of the Diving God (west view)

Temple of the Diving God

The Temple of the Diving God (Structure 5) is constructed upon an older building twenty-seven feet long and twenty feet wide which serves as the substructure for the temple. A striking feature of this temple is the outward lean or negative batter of the exterior walls. This outward slope of the exterior wall is an element of strength, for the slope of the wall tends to balance the interior projection which forms one side of the interior vault and thereby introduces the principle of the cantilever. The sides of the doorway also slope inward so that the top of the doorway is narrower than the bottom.

Temple of the Diving God from the Courtyard

The temple has a single chamber with a door facing west. The stairway is off center to the south. Above the door is a niche which contains the Diving God with wings on his arms from shoulder to elbow. The wrists and ankles are adorned with heavy rings and on the god's head is an elaborate crown. The façade of the temple below the cornice was originally decorated with mural paintings which are no longer visible.

Although the buildings at Tulum seem crude, it must be remembered that originally they were covered with stucco—sometimes with as many as twenty-seven coats—which gave a smooth finish to the rough interior. The stucco was often painted.

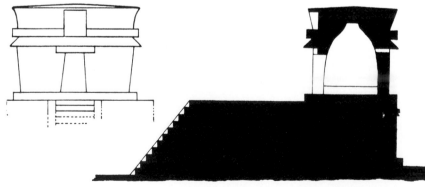

Drawings of cross-section and elevation of the Temple of the Diving God

From Lothrop, *Tulum*

220

The Diving God, Temple of the Diving God

The most common niche figure at Tulum is the Diving (or Descending) God. It is the representation of a deity with a bird's tail and with wings on his arms and shoulders and is portrayed in the act of flying downward. He holds in his hand the kan glyph of the corn god.

There are more surviving representations of the Diving God at Tulum than at any other place in Mexico. He has been described as Ahmuzencab, the diving bee. The god is represented with beelike features—the abdomen and the upper part of the body. The Diving God may also be related to Xux Ek, one form of Venus as the morning star. These two forms appear on the murals and the sculpture of Tulum (Miller, 1976: personal communication). It has also been suggested that he represents the dying sun, a conception which may be accurate when he is presented, as here, on the west side of the temple.

From Lothrop, *Tulum*

Drawing of the Diving God

221

Structure 7, Shrine

Structure 7

Structure 7 is a large shrine, ten feet square and seven feet high. There are four doorways which slope inward toward the top. Inside there is a small altar two and one-half feet square and one foot high. The diminutive size of this oratory and other structures at Tulum gave rise to the myth that Tulum was built and populated by dwarfs. It has been suggested that this and other small structures may have been used for sighting out to sea, but more likely they were simply shrines.

Structure 8

Structure 8

This square platform (twenty-seven feet by twenty-seven feet) nine feet high (Structure 8) is directly to the west of the Castillo stairway and within the ceremonial inner enclosure. The platform exhibits a rectangular molding, with a stairway on the east and west sides. Apparently the fact that there was no construction on top of the platform indicates that it was probably used for religious spectacles, dance, and drama.

Temple of the Initial Series

Temple of the Initial Series

The Temple of the Initial Series (Structure 9) is located at the southeast corner of the inner area. Immediately to the west of it is the south gateway to the ceremonial enclosure. The temple was named by Lothrop and so designated because Stephens found on the floor fragments of Stela 1. The stela once stood outside the building in the courtyard to the north. George P. Howe in 1911 deciphered the Initial Series: 9.6.10.0.0, 8 Ahau 13 Pax (A.D. 564, January 29). Arthur G. Miller's work in the Tulum area has demonstrated that the dedicatory date of the stela is not contemporaneous with any of the construction at Tulum and that it must have been moved from another site, possibly Tancah, as the stela is probably more than six hundred years older than the earliest construction at Tulum.

Structure 21

Structure 21

Structure 21 was a large flat-ceiling palace and is located immediately north of the Temple of the Frescoes. It faces south and extends from "main street" to the Inner Enclosure.

The flat ceiling is the most distinctive characteristic of east coast and Tulum architecture. Such a ceiling was formed of large wooden supporting beams laid across columns topped with masonry piers on which small poles were spread at right angles. The poles were covered with a mortar-and-rubble cap a foot or more in thickness.

Here this method of construction produced a large room 17.5 feet wide by 59 feet long. The main entrance to the building is 35 feet wide and is divided by four columns. The building was L-shaped with a wing on the west side. In addition to being used as a public building, this palace could have been used as a residential structure by the nobility.

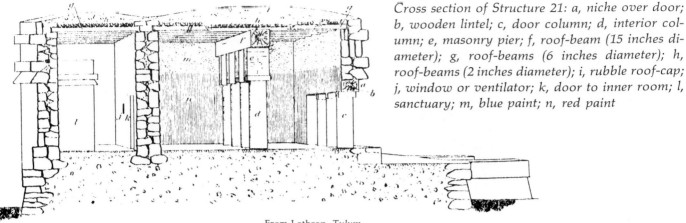

Cross section of Structure 21: a, niche over door; b, wooden lintel; c, door column; d, interior column; e, masonry pier; f, roof-beam (15 inches diameter); g, roof-beams (6 inches diameter); h, roof-beams (2 inches diameter); i, rubble roof-cap; j, window or ventilator; k, door to inner room; l, sanctuary; m, blue paint; n, red paint

From Lothrop, *Tulum*

Structure 25

This palace (Structure 25) is north of Structure 21 and faces a small courtyard to the south. It is connected to a platform (Structure 22) which joins it on its southwest corner and extends south. At the north and south ends of the platform Lothrop discovered two vaulted tombs. The tomb at the north end was partly excavated, and a few fragments of pottery were discovered.

A polychrome stucco figure of the Diving God is located in the niche above the central doorway. Originally it was painted red, blue, black, and orange. The background and some of the feathers were black, and blue and red were used on the body. The plates of the collar were painted orange, it is assumed to emulate the color of gold. On either side of the body and tail are twisted strands of cord which may represent umbilical cords and therefore birth. Two serpents emerge from the tail.

Structure 25

Diving God, Structure 25

227

Cenote House

The Cenote House (Structure 35)

The Cenote House is constructed over a small *cenote*, a limestone cave containing water. This building is next to the northeastern gate in the great wall and is a small building of the palace type. The principal façade faces away from the *cenote* and east toward the sea.

Structure 45 and Cenote House

Structure 45

Structure 45 sits on the cliff overlooking the sea. It is located across the cove from the Castillo. It faces north and overlooks the north wall and the Cenote House. Temple 45 is unique at Tulum by virtue of its circular substructure. Against the back wall is an altar which was still in use by the Mayas at the time of the work of Lothrop in 1924.

Structure 34 and Temple 45

Structure 34

Structure 34 is a palace-type structure which is located near the northwest gate in the great wall and faces west to the so-called main street of Tulum. It has a stairway with *alfardas* on either side and three doors divided by columns. Originally it had a mortar-and-rubble roof supported by wooden beams.

Watch Tower

The Watch Tower (Structure 55)

In his *Incidents of Travel in Yucatán*, first published in 1843, Stephens described his visit to Tulum, which he spelled "Tuloom." He called Structure 55 a "watch-tower," and of it he wrote: "It is twelve feet square, and has two doorways. The interior is plain, and against the back wall is a small altar, at which the guard might offer up prayers for the preservation of the city. But no guard sits in the watch-tower now; trees are growing around it; within the walls the city is desolate and overgrown, and without is an unbroken forest. The battlements, on which the proud Indian strode with his bow and arrow, and plumes of feathers, are surmounted by immense thorn bushes and overrun by poisonous vines. The city no longer keeps watch; the fiat of destruction has gone out against it, and in solitude it rests, the abode of silence and desolation (p. 271)."

Actually, the structure was probably used as a temple rather than a watch tower, although it is located at the northwest corner of the great wall.

Glossary

Alfarda. A raised sloping border to a staircase.

Basal platform. A raised, horizontal flat surface which acts as an architectural base.

Batter. The sloping face of a wall of tapered section. A wall with inverted taper, thicker at the top than at the bottom, has negative batter.

Bearing wall. A material layer usually of masonry construction which encloses space and carries the thrust of the roof load to the ground or substructure.

Capital. The uppermost member of a column; it serves as a transition from the shaft to the lintel.

Capstone. A caping stone.

Cella. A temple chamber.

Cenote. A natural well in a collapsed portion of surface limestone of Yucatán.

Chaac (Chac). God of Rain.

Chacmool. A fanciful yet standard term designating the stone figures of recumbent human males shown holding basins or platters on the abdomen (Mexico and Yucatán).

Chultun. A Maya cistern carved into the limestone bedrock or built into the stone fill of the plazas of ceremonial centers (Morley & Brainerd, 1963: 264).

Classic period. The Maya cultural period from circa A.D. 200 to 925 (Thompson, 1954: 309).

Codex (pl., *codices*). Maya native book. Only three have survived: the Codex Dresdensis, the Codex Tro-Cortesianus, and the Codex Peresianus.

Colonette. A small column.

Column. A vertical, weight-carrying architectural member, circular in cross-section, consisting of a base (sometimes omitted), a shaft, and a capital.

Corbel. A projecting wall member used as support for an element of the superstructure.

Corbel vault. A masonry projection supported by corbels and frequently connected to form a vault.

Cornice. A projection that crowns a building or wall.

Cross vault. A vault formed by the intersection of two or more simple vaults.

Curtain wall. A material layer, usually of masonry construction, which simply encloses space.

Façade. Usually, the front of a building; also, the other sides when they are emphasized architecturally.

Facude mask. A carved head or face used as ornament on the front of a building; a grotesque.

Florescent period. The greatest era of sculpture, hieroglyphic writing, and building by the lowland Mayas. Circa A.D. 625–800 (Thompson, 1954: 309).

Flying façade. Ornamental vertical extension of the façade of a Maya building.

Frieze. A scupltured or ornamented band.

Gallery. A roofed promenade; a long and narrow passage.

Glyph. A carved figure or character, incised or in relief.

Initial series. A Classic Maya method (also called long count) for dating events by the day-count from a starting point. Identified by its initial position in longer inscriptions. Each digit is vigesimal rather than decimal: in a date transcribed 9.6.10.0.0, the first digit states 9 cycles of 400 years (each having 20 periods of 20 years) have elapsed, followed by 6 twenty-year periods or katuns, 10 tuns or years of 360 days each, 0 uinals or months of 20 days each, and 0 kins or days. The total enumerates the days which have elapsed since the starting point.

Lattice work. A framework of crossed strips.

Lintel. A beam used to span an opening.

Mayanized-Mexican. The culture which emerged in Yucatán in the Post-Classic period as a result of the amalgamation of the Maya and Mexican peoples.

Milpa. A small burned clearing planted and abandoned after a few seasons.

Modified florescent period. Era of building, particularly at Chichén Itzá, which followed the Florescent or Classic period in Maya culture.

Molding. A continuous narrow surface, either projecting or recessed, plain or ornamented, whose purpose is to break up a surface, to accent, or to decorate by means of the light and dark it produces; as in cornice molding, which is the topmost molding; and medial molding, which is the second or middle molding that marks the roof edge.

Pier. A vertical, unattached masonry support.

Plinth. The lowest member of a base; also, a block serving as a base.

Portico. A porch with a roof supported by columns.

Post-Classic period. The era of Maya culture which followed the Classic period, the evidence of which is found primarily in the Yucatán area.

Puuc. A low range of limestone hills in western Yucatán south of Mérida.

Quetzal. Central American bird of brilliant plumage.

Roof comb. A structure placed on the roof of a building which resembles the comb of a cock, very often of open work.

Rubble. Rough, broken stones used in filling courses of walls.

Sacbe (pl., *sacbeob*). Maya raised artificial road.

Stela (pl., *stelae*). Sculptured stone monument.

Stepped frets. Ornamental networks sculpted in relief each offset in height and nested one within the other.

Substructure. Undercarriage; groundwork.

Terrace. A raised, open platform usually with steeply sloping sides.

Vault. An arched structure of masonry usually forming a ceiling or roof.

Weight-releasing device. Open fenestration which directs the thrust from the load of the roof through the bearing wall.

Appendix I: Key to Pronunciation

Maya pronunciation of vowels as in Spanish*: *a*, between that of *rat* and *rather*; *e*, between that in *pet* and *pray*, but short; *i* as *ee* in *greed*; *o* as in *on*; *u* like our *oo* as in *boo*, but pronounced as *w* before another vowel.

Consonants as in English except that *c* is always hard; *x* as *sh*, so *uix* is pronounced *weesh*. *Qu* is pronounced like *k* before *e* and *i*; consonants followed by an apostrophe are pronounced with a quick closing of the glottis, somewhat as in military commands—*shun* for *attention*. Final *e* is always pronounced.

Examples

Chichén Itzá	Chee-chen´ EE-tza´
Uxmal	Oosh-mal´
Labná	Lab-na´
Xlapak	Shla-pak´
Ahau	A-how´

*From J. Eric S. Thompson, *The Rise and Fall of Maya Civilization* (Norman, 1954, 1966), xv. Used by permission of the University of Oklahoma Press.

Appendix II: Maya Architectural Terms Illustrated

The architectural terms used in the text and defined
in the glossary are illustrated here.

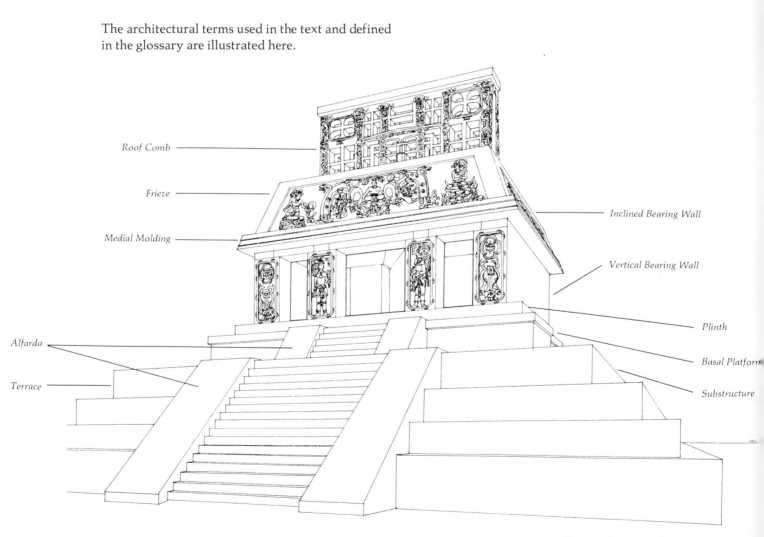

Roof Comb

Frieze

Inclined Bearing Wall

Medial Molding

Vertical Bearing Wall

Plinth

Alfarda

Basal Platform

Terrace

Substructure

Temple of the Sun (Restoration), Palenque

From G. F. Andrews, *Maya Cities*

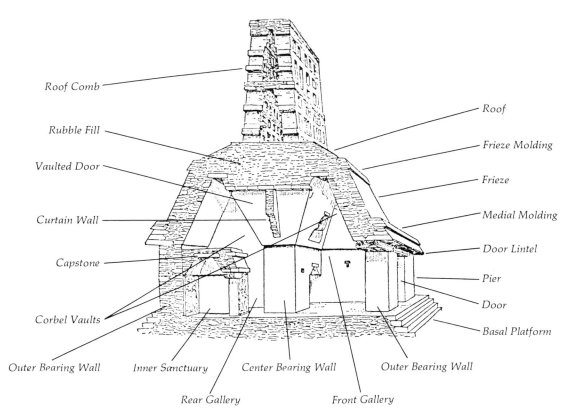

Roof Comb

Rubble Fill

Vaulted Door

Curtain Wall

Capstone

Corbel Vaults

Outer Bearing Wall

Inner Sanctuary

Center Bearing Wall

Outer Bearing Wall

Rear Gallery

Front Gallery

Roof

Frieze Molding

Frieze

Medial Molding

Door Lintel

Pier

Door

Basal Platform

From Thompson, The Rise and Fall of Maya Civilization

Temple of the Cross, Palenque

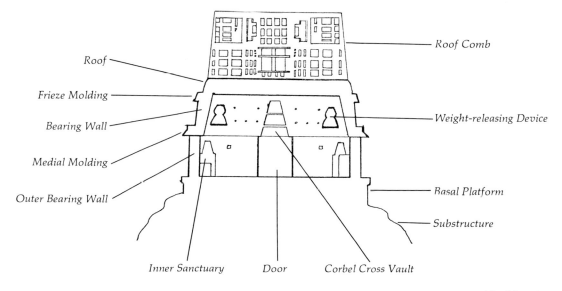

Roof

Frieze Molding

Bearing Wall

Medial Molding

Outer Bearing Wall

Roof Comb

Weight-releasing Device

Basal Platform

Substructure

Inner Sanctuary

Door

Corbel Cross Vault

After Marquina

Temple of the Cross, Palenque

237

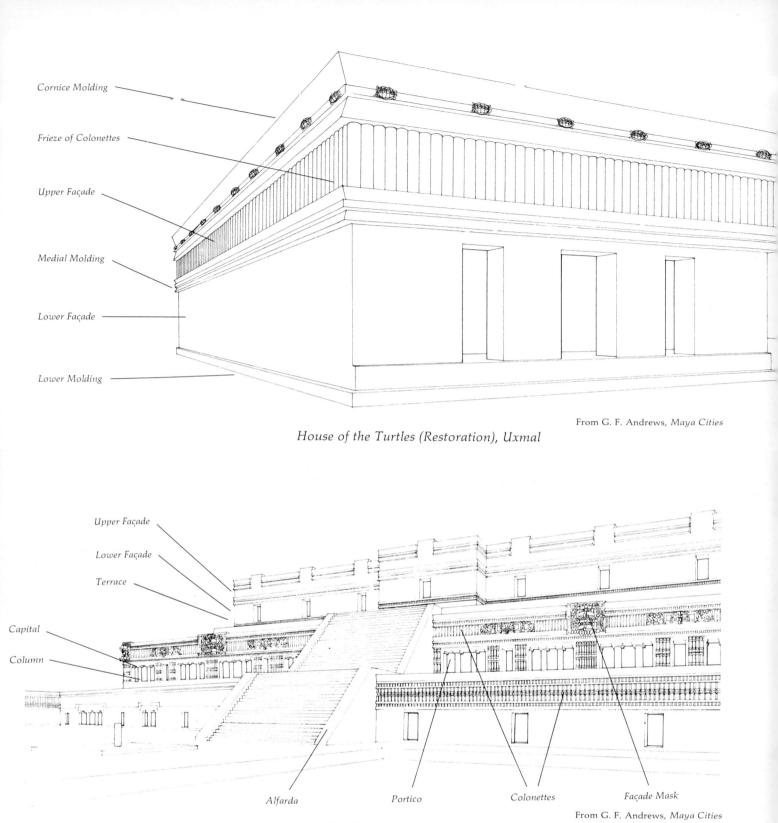

Cornice Molding

Frieze of Colonettes

Upper Façade

Medial Molding

Lower Façade

Lower Molding

From G. F. Andrews, *Maya Cities*

House of the Turtles (Restoration), Uxmal

Upper Façade

Lower Façade

Terrace

Capital

Column

Alfarda

Portico

Colonettes

Façade Mask

From G. F. Andrews, *Maya Cities*

The Palace (Restoration), Sayil

238

North Colonnade (Restoration), Chichén Itzá
From Proskouriakoff, *An Album of Maya Architecture*

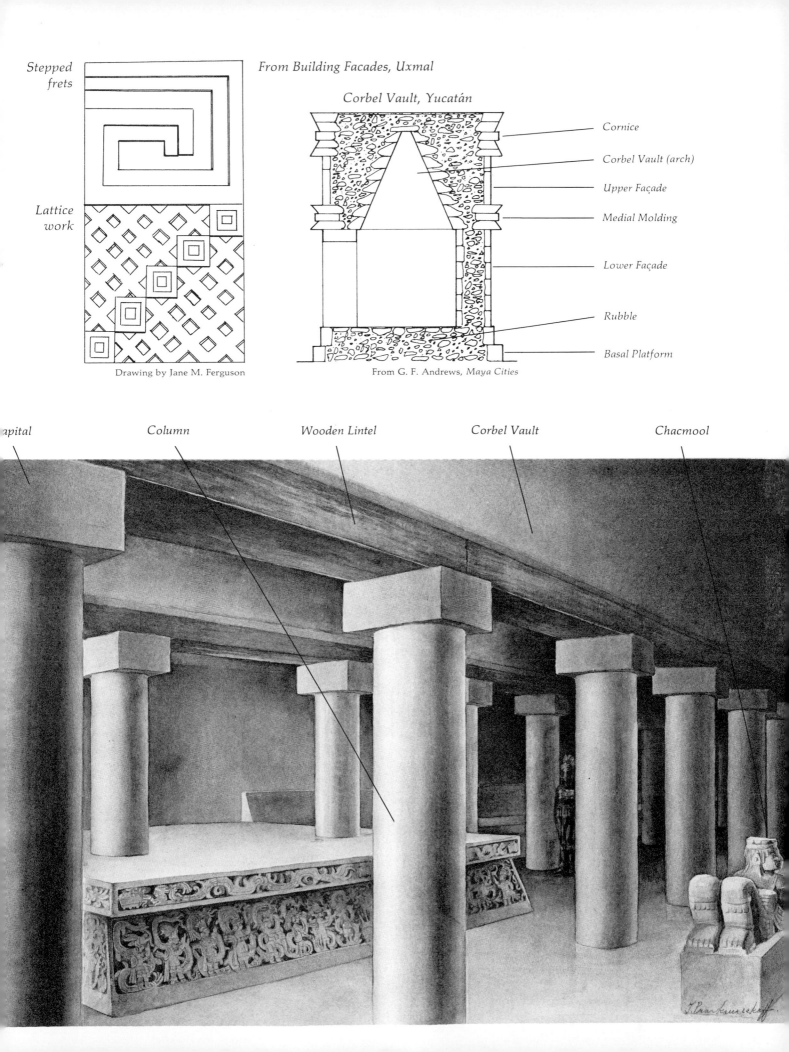

Stepped frets

Lattice work

From Building Facades, Uxmal

Corbel Vault, Yucatán

Cornice

Corbel Vault (arch)

Upper Façade

Medial Molding

Lower Façade

Rubble

Basal Platform

Drawing by Jane M. Ferguson

From G. F. Andrews, *Maya Cities*

Capital   Column   Wooden Lintel   Corbel Vault   Chacmool

Appendix III: Kings of Palenque

465 A.D.	birth of Cauac-Uinal I	9. 1.10. 0. 0	
490	birth of Hok	9. 2.15. 3. 8	
501	accession of Cauac-Uinal I	9. 3. 6. 7.17	5 Caban 0 Zotz
514	House D, pier b date in eaves	9. 4. 0. 0. 0	
523	birth of Cauac-Uinal II	9. 4. 9. 0. 4	
524	birth of Bahlum	9. 4.10. 1. 5	
	death of Cauac-Uinal I	9. 4.10. 4.17	5 Caban 5 Mac
528	accession of Hok	9. 4.14.10. 4	5 Kan 12 Kayab
565	death of Hok	9. 6.11. 0.16	7 Cib 4 Kayab
	accession of Cauac-Uinal II	9. 6.11. 5. 1	1 Imix 4 Zip
570	death of Cauac-Uinal II	9. 6.16.10. 7	9 Manik 5 Yaxkin
572	accession of Bahlum	9. 6.18. 5. 2	10 Eb 0 Uo
582	death of Bahlum	9. 7. 9. 5. 5	11 Chicchan 3 Kayab
583	accession of Lady Kan-Ik	9. 7.10. 3. 8	9 Lamat 1 Muan
603	birth of Pacal the Great	9. 8. 9.13. 0	8 Ahau 13 Pop
604	death of Lady Kan-Ik	9. 8.11. 6.12	2 Eb 20 Ceh (0 Mac)
	accession of Aahc-Kan	9. 8.11. 9.10	8 Oc 18 Muan
611	death of Pacal 1st	9. 8.18.14.11	3 Chuen 4 Uayeb
612	death of Aahc-Kan	9. 8.19. 4. 6	2 Cimi 14 Mol
	accession of Lady Zac-Kuk	9. 8.19. 7.18	9 Etz'nab 6 Ceh
615	accession of Lord Shield Pacal	9. 9. 2. 4. 8	5 Lamat 1 Mol
635	birth of Chan-Bahlum	9.10. 2. 6. 6	2 Cimi 19 Zotz'
640	death of Lady Zac-Kuk	9.10. 7.13. 5	4 Chicchan 13 Yax
642	death of Bahlum Mo'o	9.10.10. 1. 6	13 Cimi 4 Pax
643	birth of Hok	9.10.11.17. 0	11 Ahau 8 Mac
670	birth of Chac Zutz'	9.11.18. 9.17	7 Caban 15 Kayab
678	birth of Chaac	9.12. 6. 5. 8	3 Lamat 7 Zac
683	death of Lord Shield Pacal	9.12.11. 5.18	6 Etz'nab 11 Yax
	accession of Chan-Bahlum	9.12.11.12.10	8 Oc 3 Kayab
701	death of Chan-Bahlum	9.13.10. 1. 5	6 Chicchan 3 Pop
	accession of Hok	9.13.10. 6. 8	5 Lamat 6 Xul
719	death of Hok	Post 9.14. 9.14.15	9 Men 3 Yax
721	accession of Chaac	9.14.10. 4. 2	9 Ik 5 Kayab
722	accession of Chac Zutz'	9.14.11.12.14	8 Ix 7 Yaxkin
731	death of Chac Zutz'	Post 9.15. 0. 0. 0	4 Ahau 13 Yax
764	accession of Kuk	9.16.13. 0. 7	9 Manik 15 Uo
783 post	death of Kuk	Post 9.17.13. 0. 7	7 Manik 0 Pax

Source: After Lounsbury 1974: 6; 1975 and Mathews and Schele 1974: 72; from Robertson 1974.

References

Andrews, E. Wyllys
  1965 "Archaeology and Prehistory in the Northern Maya Lowlands: An Introduction," *Handbook of Middle American Indians*, Volume 2. Austin.
Andrews, George F.
  1975 *Maya Cities: Place Making and Urbanization*. Norman.
Bolles, John S.
  1977 *Las Monjas: A Major Pre-Mexican Architectural Complex at Chichén Itzá*. Norman.
Coe, Michael D.
  1966 *The Maya*. New York.
  1968 *America's First Civilization*. New York.
Cohodas, Marvin
  1973 "The Iconography of the Panels of the Sun, Cross, and Foliated Cross at Palenque," *Primera Mesa Redonda de Palenque*, Part II, p. 95. Pebble Beach.
Hammond, Norman
  1977 "The Earliest Maya" Scientific American, March, 1977, Vol. 236, No. 3.
Kowalski, Jeff.
  1976 Personal Communication
Kubler, George
  1975 *Art and Architecture of Ancient America*, second edition. Baltimore.
La Fay, Howard
  1975 "The Maya, Children of Time," *National Geographic*, Vol. 148, No. 6.
Lothrop, S. K.
  1924 *Tulum, An Archaeological Study of the East Coast of Yucatán*. Washington.
Miller, Arthur G.
  1976a. Personal communication.
  1976b. "Captains of the Itzá: Unpublished Mural Evidence from Chichén Itzá." In *Social Process in Maya Prehistory: Studies in Memory of Sir Eric Thompson*. Academic Press Inc. (London) Ltd. In press.

  1976c. "The Little Descent: Manifest Destiny from the East." Paper delivered in symposium, "Highland Culture Contact in the Lowland Maya Area: Recent Data and Implications," 42d International Congress of Americanists, Paris, September 2–9, 1976.
Morley, Sylvanus G.
  1963 *The Ancient Maya*. Revised by George W. Brainerd. Stanford.
Proskouriakoff, Tatiana
  1963 *An Album of Maya Architecture*. Norman.
Ruz L' Huillier, Alberto
  1974 *Uxmal, Official Guide*. Mexico. D.F.
  1976 *Chichén Itzá, Official Guide*. Mexico, D.F.
Schele, Linda
  1976 Personal Communication.
Stephens, John Lloyd
  1963 *Incidents of Travel in Yucatán*. New York. First published, 1843. Also republished by the University of Oklahoma Press, 1962.
Thompson, J. Eric S.
  1954 *The Rise and Fall of Maya Civilization*. Norman. Second edition, enlarged, 1966.
  1963 *Maya Archaeologist*. Norman.
Robertson, Merle Greene, editor
  1974 The Art, Iconography, & Dynastic History of Palenque, Part III. Pebble Beach, California.
  ———, Harry E. D. Pollock, and Jean Charlot
  1932 *A Preliminary Study of the Ruins of Cobá, Quintana Roo, Mexico*. Washington.
Tozzer, Alfred M.
  1957 "Chichén Itzá and its Cenote of Sacrifice," *Memoirs of the Peabody Museum of Archaeology and Ethnology*, Vols, 11–12. Cambridge, Mass.
  1941 "Landa's Relacion De Las Cosas De Yucatan," Papers of the Peabody Museum of Archaeology and Ethnology, Harvard University, Vol. XVIII. Cambridge, Mass.

Index